Welcome to the USSA

Welcome to the USSA

◆

Corruption in the government and media

Unearthing the Neocon Camarilla

Ryan Dawson

iUniverse, Inc.
New York Lincoln Shanghai

Welcome to the USSA
Corruption in the government and media

iUniverse books may be ordered through booksellers or by contacting:

iUniverse
2021 Pine Lake Road, Suite 100
Lincoln, NE 68512
www.iuniverse.com
1-800-Authors (1-800-288-4677)

ISBN-13: 978-0-595-39384-8 (pbk)
ISBN-13: 978-0-595-83783-0 (ebk)
ISBN-10: 0-595-39384-5 (pbk)
ISBN-10: 0-595-83783-2 (ebk)

Printed in the United States of America

Contents

1

Is the USA becoming the U$A?
What Happened to America?

o o o o o o o o o o o o o o o o o o o o o o o o o o o o o o o o o o o o

"But that's OK, if this were a dictatorship would be a heck of a lot easier, just so long as I'm the dictator"

—*George W. Bush[1]*

If America was headed in the direction of an imperialist, plutocratic, police state what would it look like? Ask yourself what steps would the government take to create such a political machine? Would there be an attack on the civil liberties? Would there be a power shift into the executive branch? Would the Supreme Court ignore blatant violations of the Bill of Rights? Would the government engage in domestic spying? Would the 4th and 5th amendments be washed away with unconstitutional legislation such as the PATRIOT Acts? Would the government have the ability to control our property, would they suspend immanent domain for private interests? Would the government openly engage in torture and even go as far as attempting to legalize it? Would companies with business ties to government employees receive the benefits of our tax dollars or worse yet money borrowed from private banks who charge interest? Would the government secretly build massive concentration camps and hire Halliburton to do it? Would our military be treated like a toy and thrown into conflicts based on fabricated evidence and fear-mongering?

---

1.   George Bush December 18, 2000. CNN transcript here http://transcripts.cnn.com/
      TRANSCRIPTS/0012/18/nd.01.html Video footage here http://www.
      newsgateway.ca/bush_dictator.htm

What role would the media play? Would we reach a point where polls would show that people turning to comedy channels had more accurate information than people who watched mainstream televised news media such as Fox News as their primary source? To go further, would over half of the mainstream news viewers actually believe in outright distortions? Would the country have a presidential election between two pro-war candidates, even when over half the country was anti-war, and hundreds of thousands of people took to the streets in major US cities to protest? Would over half the country's discretionary taxes go to military spending? Would the president make jokes about how things would be easier if he was a dictator? Would corporate scandals like Enron and World-Com be raging out of control? Could the FBI catch a foreign government spying on the US, through the defense department, with officials from an overwhelmingly powerful lobby and the televised press not talk about it? Would officials in the administration purposely leak information about our own CIA agents stifling their ability to track nuclear weapons proliferation in order to cover the administration's own conscious disinformation of their pre-invasion intelligence on Iraq's alleged activities? Could a super Zionist and super lobbyist like Jack Abarmoff conspire to swindle tens of millions away from American Indians[2] and use the money to bribe members of congress and support[3] Israeli's Jew only racial colonies' violent illegal military occupation of Palestine?

If the country was heading towards a plutocracy, would free market capitalism give way to state assisted monopolies? Communism is State control of industry. It's not a form of government, it's a economic system concerning the of means of production and distribution. What do we call the hundreds of billions of tax payer dollars freely given by the government to select industries, if not communism? Industries get money from the state in many crafty ways from earmarked foreign aid to farm subsidies abuse to no-bid contracts. Could British papers report that the president's grandfather Prsecott Bush has been confirmed[4] as the director of a firm that helped finance the Nazis and continued to do so even after America entered the war?

Could the president's father have financed the mujahedeen which became the Taliban and continues to have numerous relationships with the Bin Laden family? Is this the USSA? People all of these things have already happened. What was G. W. Bush's father doing on the morning of September 11th and who was he

---

2.   http://www.washingtonpost.com/wp-dyn/content/graphic/2005/12/12/
     GR2005121200286.html

3.   http://www.msnbc.msn.com/id/7615249/site/newsweek/

4.   http://www.guardian.co.uk/usa/story/0,12271,1312540,00.html

with? He was meeting with Osama bin Laden's brother, Shafig bin Laden, in the Ritz-Carlton Hotel.

What really happened on 911? Does the government lie? Have they lied before? Have conspiracies worked in the past? Is questioning the events around 911 really just for the tinfoil hats crowd? Has the government ever carried out large secret operations before as they did with Iran Contra or the assassination of democratically elected political leaders like President Salvador Allende of Chili which occurred on September 11th 1973? How could the 911 commission not even address the collapse of one of the buildings, building number 7 which was not hit by a plane and has every physical indication of a demolition? Why are officials from both the Bush and Reagan administration coming out and saying 911 was an inside job? Why has the government of Venezuela launched a new 911 investigation? If it is only crazy people who question 911 then why did CNN's own poll, of over fifty thousand people, show that 83% agreed that the government's official story is a cover up? Raymond McGovern served seven US presidents over 27 years as a CIA analyst and operations officer. He has pointedly said that 911 was an inside job. Andreas von Bülow Former German Secretary Of Defense has openly stated he believes that 911 was carried out by a faction inside the US government. R.M. Bowman the director of Advanced Space Programs Development, which was later, coined "StarWars," in the Reagan administration, and a United States Air Force Lieutenant Colonel has publicly stated that 911 was an inside job. There is a long list of government officials and scholars who question what happened on 911 but where is their voice?

Why isn't the media doing its supposed job? Why did bloggers who had far less resources than the mainstream media, get the facts right about Iraq? Could it be because our press actively helped to mislead the citizenry? Does the media lie? Have they been caught hyping up whoppers in the past like Y2K and SARS? How much coverage did the crisis in the Sudan get compared to say Michael Jackson's trial? How much coverage has the AIPAC spy ring gotten compared to say the Lacey Peterson case or distasteful cartoons? Has anyone seen the media's cartoon portrayals of the Japanese during WWII? Is it not a common historical trend to dehumanize the enemies of the state?

Why has the press and the government made so many mistakes? Is America following the path of the USSR? America is engaged in simultaneous perpetual wars, and the Bush administration has driven up the national debt more over $8,000,000,000,000.00 more than all the debts of the previous presidents combined. Can we see the writing on the wall? What has happened to Empires in the past which have taken this same route? Are we headed towards an economic collapse? Is the war on terror a cover for a war for global hegemony with the US on the throne? Are we fostering terrorism by engaging in it ourselves? Does our congress represent American interests or the bidding of the wealthy and the lobbyists? Would Rumsfeld and Cheney set up a shadow government called the Office of Special Plans comprised of die hard Zionists who follow a plan for global domination outlined in a document call Project for a New American Century which was based on policy papers from a foreign government which enjoys a hand in glove relationship with billionaire religious institutions and a unique position to channel money into the military industrial complex? How did this all happen? Who did it and how? Who is to blame? What is wrong with our system of government, our press, and our culture? What can we do to fix it? America is not America any more. If we do not stand up soon, if we do not get active soon, the lies and the killings will continue and America could quite possibly create the beginning of WWIII and there will be no winners of that war.

First thing we have to do is realize how we got in to this mess, and do away with this blame it all on Bush attitude. This debacle has been created with the sheep like submissiveness of congress and the courts to the puppet masters who make monkey George dance at their bidding. Our entire system needs an overhaul. It's time the government start fearing the people rather than the people being led by fear created by the government.

2

Know Your Enemy The Neocons

○ ○
"Ye shall know the truth, and the truth shall make you mad."

—Aldous Huxley

Political and media corruption go far beyond Bush. Drop the two-party paradigm for a bit and acknowledge what is going on in the United States. If you are sick of unjust wars and an imperialist America, then it is vital to recognize who the Neo-conservatives are. We call them Neocons. A disproportionate amount of Neocons are, in title, Republicans. They are not conservatives; as they break from the two core principles of real conservative ideology; less government and fiscal responsibility. The Neocons appear to be a mesh of the worst elements from both major parties. It is the fanatically religious right joining forces with the pro big government left to make one hell of a messed up party, masking as "Republicans" or "compassionate conservatives." But make no mistake about it. The Democrats also have their share of Neocons, such as Lieberman, Hillary, and Kerry to name a few. The Neocons obey a certain lobby ahead of any partisan lines. Regardless of their party the Neocons are uniform on their positions on the wars in the Middle East and their support for the fascist actions of the Israeli government.

Get a comfortable chair and maybe something to throw because most of the things in this book are not going to be found inside a classroom text book and certainly not on the evening news. You will become angry, you will be outraged, and you will be disturbed.

No topics are sacred here. We're going to kick around religions, political parties, Israel, the military, and everything else you're told not to talk about. We're going to get into the media, hyper consumerism, corporate government, the recent wars and the accompanying deceptions that the mass media ignored, and the roll of what I call the 'Big 4' ~ Energy, Agribusiness, Pharmaceuticals, and Weapons industries. So it has been said that I don't push buttons, I dance on them. But people must break through the emotional hissy-fits constructed around these topics if they are ever to come close to scraping their way out of the cave. The MIC[1], the nasty camarilla of the OSP[2], MSM[3], NWO[4], and the Neo-cons in the two major political parties do not want you to have this information. We shall remove the rose colored glasses, the sugar coating and the 'nothing but blue skies smiling at me,' fixation of America and take a hard look at our government and the growing bloody reality of imperialism. Everything is not roses, sugar, and blue skies. (Red White and Blue.)

The governing bodies of the good old USA are full of as much corruption and deception as the old USSR. Our Civil Liberties are being attacked from all sides thanks to a heavy dose of hollow scare tactics. Free speech is now being designated into "free speech zones." And rather than actually having a voice, people are caged away and virtually ignored by the press. The courts now allow the government property seizures[5] for the use of private enterprise. The PATRIOT Act allows for a dictator's wet dream. It grants the government the ability to evade due process of law and hold political dissidents in detention indefinitely based on any vague definition of national security. Bush tried to join Israel[6] by attempting to make the US the only other country on earth with legalized[7] torture.[8] When that failed, they aimed at exemptions for the CIA and private contractors to continue the barbaric practice. To top it all off, our president has allowed the government to ignore the 4th amendment and spy on the American public by eavesdropping on our phone calls without going to a court or receiving a warrant. Our constitution is only a piece of paper if we do not enforce it. As far as the Neocons are concerned, it might as well be a piece of toilet paper.[9]

Our republican experiment is flailing like imperial nations from the past. We are enmeshed in the same Plutocratic trappings which tore apart the Greek republics of ancient times, and the same over expanded and banker-ruled failings

---

1.   Military Industrial Complex
2.   Office of Special Plans a cabal under Cheney and Rumsfeld
3.   Main Stream Media
4.   New World Order
5.   http://www.washingtonpost.com/wp-dyn/content/article/2005/06/23/AR2005062300783_pf.html
6.   http://news.bbc.co.uk/1/hi/world/americas/1781577.stm
7.   http://news.bbc.co.uk/1/hi/world/middle_east/637293.stm

of Rome and Spain. A plutocracy[10] is a democracy's natural end if the public does not or cannot maintain an active participation (due to a lack of media) in the activities of the government. John Stewart Mills, the father of Utilitarian philosophy and woman's suffrage advocate, claimed that a democracy could only work insofar as its public was educated and tolerant. Both of these qualities are predicated by a proper access to information, without which we can have neither. Our press is bribed, censored, and threatened. Some 'news' comes straight from the pentagon. Our congress is quite openly bribed and beholden to special interests. Jack Abramoff is just the tip of the iceberg. We have a problem with the system whereby ethics are replaced by dollar bills and selling a war to the public is frighteningly akin to promoting a consumer product.

We are at war with Iraq because of a Zionist cabal embedded in the Defense Department, called the Office of Special Plans or the OSP. The war party has flip-flopped its reasons for the war several times. But as the emotional smoke clears and the ranting and raving dies down, all we have are "mistaken" intelligence and "miscalculations." To which they ignore responsibility and cry "We must stay the course." They dream of perpetual war, and through that, perpetual profiteering, erosion of Civil Liberties, and a consolidation of power. But, understand this, without the complacent media, they would have no chance.

The truth, which the main stream media will not tell you, is that the war with Iraq was a conscious decision planned well before 911 in a document called

---

8. *Torture.* "From 1967," Amnesty reports, "the Israeli security services have routinely tortured Palestinian political suspects in the Occupied Territories." B'Tselem found that eighty-five percent of Palestinians interrogated by Israeli security services were subjected to "methods constituting torture," while already a decade ago Human Rights Watch estimated that "the number of Palestinians tortured or severely illtreated" was "in the tens of thousands—a number that becomes especially significant when it is remembered that the universe of adult and adolescent male Palestinians in the West Bank and Gaza is under three-quarters of one million." In 1987 Israel became "the only country in the world to have effectively legalized torture" (Amnesty). Although the Israeli Supreme Court seemed to ban torture in a 1999 decision, the Public Committee Against Torture in Israel reported in 2003 that Israeli security forces continued to apply torture in a "methodical and routine" fashion. A 2001 B'Tselem study documented that Israeli security forces often applied "severe torture" to "Palestinian minors." http://www.normanfinkelstein. com/article.php?pg=11&ar=130 Norman G. Finkelstein

9. Bush on the Constitution: 'It's just a goddamned piece of paper' By Doug Thompson Dec 9, 2005, 07:53 http://www.capitolhillblue.com/artman/publish/article_7779.shtml

PNAC, Project for a New American Century. PNAC's was based on[11] some Israeli policy papers[12] written for former Prime Minister Benjamin Netanyahu. This document is like a modern <u>Mein Kampf.</u>[13] They say how and what they are going to do, and then they do it. PNAC calls for a war with Iraq. The road to Damascus runs through Baghdad[14] it alluded, yet it openly states that the public would not support such a war plan, short of "…some kind of catastrophic catalyzing event,—like a new Pearl Harbor."[15] *[Something like Nine Eleven…]*

The co-authors of PNAC overlap with the people in the Bush administration who made the deceiving case for war in Iraq, and who have connections to Israel and unconditional hard-line Zionism. There is a common tie in all the scandals, fear-mongering, and lying. From PNAC to 9/11 to Plame to AIPAC to Abramoff to the Niger forgeries; the shared thread is Zionism.

Currently there are merging court cases concerning a busted Israeli spy ring inside the US, and a scandal where a CIA agent was ousted which resulted in the uncovering of her front company Brewster-Jennings & Associates, thus dismantling our ability to track nuclear weapons proliferation. Inside this case is the issue of some known forged documents that claimed Saddam was trying to buy yellowcake uranium from Niger. All of these cases, the Niger forgeries, the AIPAC[16]

---

10. A **plutocracy** is a <u>form of government</u> where all the state's decisions are centralized in an affluent wealthy class of citizenry, and the degree of <u>economic inequality</u> is high while the level of <u>social mobility</u> is low. This can apply to a multitude of government systems, as the key elements of plutocracy transcend and often occur concomitantly with the features of those systems. The word "plutocracy" itself is derived from the ancient Greek root *ploutos*, meaning wealth.—
http://en.wikipedia.org/wiki/Plutocracy
11. http://www.itszone.co.uk/zone0/viewtopic.php?t=38168
12. A Clean Break: A New Strategy for Securing the Realm http://www.iasps.org/strat1.htm
13. http://en.wikipedia.org/wiki/Mein_Kampf
14. "The Israelis, and their American amen corner, have always understood that the road to Damascus runs through Baghdad. As the authors of "A Clean Break" presciently put it:
    "*Syria enters this conflict with potential weaknesses: Damascus is too preoccupied with dealing with the threatened new regional equation to permit distractions of the Lebanese flank. And Damascus fears that the 'natural axis' with Israel on one side, central Iraq and Turkey on the other, and Jordan, in the center would squeeze and detach Syria from the Saudi Peninsula. For Syria, this could be the prelude to a redrawing of the map of the Middle East which would threaten Syria's territorial integrity.*""
    http://www.antiwar.com/justin/j050703.html 6th paragraph from the bottom.

(American Israel Public Affairs Committee) spy ring, and the outing of the clandestine CIA agent and consequently her front company and associates, tie together and trace back to the OSP, the flag ship of PNAC's planners.

The goal of the Israeli spying, based on the information they stole, was to get the U.S. to confront Iran, the only challenge to Israel's total supremacy in the Middle East. Sadly, things seem to be going according to plan. However the trial for Steve Rosen AIPAC's former top advisor and Keith Weissman, formerly AIPAC's Middle East policy expert has been set for Late April 2006 (This date has since been moved to late May 23d 2006 and is expected to be pushed back again) Americans can bet that the Neocons will go into hyper mode with the Iran propaganda to race the US into another war before the trial reveals the hidden cabal. They are desperate. These cases will reveal the real culprits. The Zionist camarilla that has manipulated the U.S. for its own relentless, power quest which has overlapping interest with the military industrial complex and its host of banking leeches.

The Neocons are shameless in their hubris and serial lying. The criminal spies in the DOD were working for Israel, which has a history of undermining our nuclear deterrents, engaging in false flag operations, and spying on the US. The maelstrom of trigger words that Israel and the US use to mask their campaign of aggression, ethnic cleansing, and neo-colonialism cannot hide them forever. Behind the cloak of religion, accusations of anti-Semitism, false claims about their enemies and the out right blame-shifting of their past manipulations, the Neocons foster the Military Industrial Complex's best cash cow: the **Israeli occupation** and the ensuing related conflicts it creates. There is a chess game over the world's energy resources, a concentration of wealth via quasi-communism, and therefore a consolidation of power by what can best be called the New World Order. We cannot let the MIC (Military Industrial complex) continue to be a medium for profiteering and serve as an amoral corporate faction over the world's people.

Bush and company are trying to shuck the blame of the war in Iraq from themselves to bad intelligence from the CIA and MI6. This is to be used as a pretext to cut up the CIA and give the administration even more power. The truth is that the bad intelligence came from the OSP, not the CIA. The faked and forged

---

15. Rebuilding America's Defenses: Strategy, Forces and Resources For a New Century A Report of the Project for the New American Century, September 2000 http:// www.newamericancentury.org/RebuildingAmericasDefenses.pdf p63

16. American Israel Public Affairs Committee, this is Israel's largest lobbying group. And the second largest lobby in the US behind AARP.

'intelligence' came from a clique inside the DOD, effectively a shadow govern-ment, the Office of Special Plans. The OSP was headed up under Donald Rums-feld and Richard Cheney by Richard Perle, who resigned[17]; Douglas Feith who has also resigned[18]; and by Lewis 'Scooter' Libby who has since resigned[19] after he was indicted[20] for being involved in the Plame Affair, which is tied to the Niger Forgeries. Larry Franklin, an Israeli mole, began his trial on Jan 3rd. It will be interesting to see how it all unfolds. Hopefully America is turning a corner and the Neocons's world is finally falling apart. Interestingly, Libby's trial has been postponed until Jan 2007 after the congressional elections. It could prove to force Cheney to resign. The Libby trial and the AIPAC trial will prove to be the Neo-con's undoing. But we have a race against time. How many more lives will be wasted in the Middle East in the Zionists' and central bankers' wet dream of per-petual war, before we can bring these nasty, blood for profit, sadists to justice?

Richard Perle and Douglas Feith are both staunch Zionists. Perle has a history of spying for Israel and Feith has been accused of it. Both so happened to resign after the FBI raided AIPAC. One can bet that Lewis Libby did not act alone, because the OSP was set up under Cheney and Rumsfeld. Ousting Valerie Plame was necessary in order to prevent accurate knowledge about Iran. The Neocons want another war for Israel and they are just as willing to create room for decep-tion about Iran as they flagrantly and shamelessly lied about Iraq. It's time Amer-icans put a stop to this. It is time to expose these players and their methods.

Politicians have the public distracted with pre-constructed arguing factions who deter the public from preventing and making known the real problems inherent in the American system, macro culture, and economic practices. The left and right serve like arms on the same monster. Within both parties are Neocons. Neocons have no loyalty to the US, they serve corporations and theology with no ties to the best interests of American people. They are utterly unconcerned with humanity. These men and women are among the sickest people on earth, advo-cating torture, indiscriminate killing of civilians, exploitation in all its nasty forms, and adopting a Leon Strauss-style-justification for lying to get their ends. The sheer inhumanity of their actions and the audacity of their devilish greed are hard for normal functioning people to fathom. The Neocons are so far removed from how sane, healthy people think and feel that it is as if one were watching

---

17.   http://www.cnn.com/2003/US/03/27/perle.resigns/

18.   http://irishantiwar.org/news/item.tcl?news_item_id=101140

19.   http://news.bbc.co.uk/1/hi/world/americas/4386748.stm

20.   http://www.boston.com/news/nation/washington/articles/2005/10/29/cheney_aide_indicted/

monsters rather than fellow human beings. These people are shameless Machiavellians who whip up a feverish militancy by attaching their cause (through lies and propaganda) to the terrible tragedy of September 11th. Riding on the unquestioning insecure wave of resentment and need for revenge, the Neocons have hijacked US foreign policy and alienated the US's long standing allies. The United States' respect around the world has been replaced with a loathing disgust, hatred, and disdain for America and a breeding ground for terrorists.

How did they do it, and what are their future plans with Iran and Syria? Perpetual war is their stated goal.

"The foreign strategy of the US must be "unapologetic, idealistic, assertive and well funded. America must not only be the world's policeman or its sheriff, it must be its beacon and guide...Our first objective is to prevent the re-emergence of a new rival. This is a dominant consideration underlying the new regional defense strategy and requires that we endeavor to prevent any hostile power from dominating a region whose resources would, under consolidated control, be sufficient to generate global power. These regions include Western Europe, East Asia, the territory of the former Soviet Union, and Southwest Asia...There are three additional aspects to this objective: First the U.S must show the leadership necessary to establish and protect a new order that holds the promise of convincing potential competitors that they need not aspire to a greater role or pursue a more aggressive posture to protect their legitimate interests. Second, in the non-defense areas, we must account sufficiently for the interests of the advanced industrial nations to discourage them from challenging our leadership or seeking to overturn the established political and economic order. Finally, we must maintain the mechanisms for deterring potential competitors from even aspiring to a larger regional or global role." [21]

Ladies and gentlemen, welcome to the USSA. Discover the true governing bodies which are hidden in plain view behind the literally deadly silence of the corporate controlled mass media. Why do people allow mass murder so long as there is a colorful banner over head?

---

21.   *—Defense Planning Guidance developed in 1992 by Paul Wolfowitz, endorsed as PNAC ideology and now established Bush foreign policy."*

3

Let's Do talk about Religion and Politics
The Historical Stupidity of War

We should be supporting Humanity not Flags

o o o o o o o o o o o o o o o o o o o o o o o o o o o o o o o o o

"War does not determine who is right—only who is left

—*Bertrand Russell"*

"Wars are inevitable…as long as we believe that wars are inevitable. The moment we don't believe it anymore it is not inevitable."

—*Lydia Sicher*

Political and religious affiliations have become emotional in-groups, divorced from philosophy entirely, and replaced with rationalization. Party members and religious tenets live in a polarized world of end-all end-alls. People no longer think of what is just and then act; they act first and then think of how they can justify it. Sadly, the driving values held up by our culture on which we base the judgment of our government's performance is economic growth and feel good macho-ism. Humanity has become an inconvenience in the way of the consolidation of power and wealth. War is stupid.

Sun Tzu said war was part of man, and at a young age it is easy for one to also believe that war is inevitable. That's before realizing how impossible war would be, were it not for the duped herd devoting themselves to the State's leaders, whose authority rests in supernatural superstitions of divinity or a crazed nationalism wrapped tightly around either xenophobia, racism, or deception. After all, one can imagine that serfdom and slavery in the past must have seemed inevitable, too. Cross culturally, these things were long standing common practices, however societies have proven these ills are not a natural byproduct of mankind but a preventable consequence derived from specific cultures. War is not pre-destined by our make up.

The reason preventable pollution, debt slavery, sanction-induced starvation, military occupation, etc. continue is because it is profitable for the corporations who rent the law makers and own the media. War and torture are excused by the lies that they are necessary. It is vicarious power for the frightened and powerless, so they buy it.

For many, truth is not based on reality. Truth is based on whatever is psychologically gratifying. Some say that stupidity is to blame. However it does not stem so much from a person's lack of intelligence as from a flaw in their moral character. The herd is formed by their lowest common insecurities. The herd is lead by the worst of the worst.

Fear makes false hope easier to swallow. Jealousy and resentment hide behind moral indignation. They color themselves as protection, security, safety, and inevitability. War is a mass of strangers killing other strangers; it's nationalism at its worst. Demand that the greedy old men fight each other instead. "Chicken hawks", to paraphrase Galloway, will always fight to the last drop of other people's blood. What historically is war?

War: *"the inhumane use of force for illegal ends justified by lies told by sociopaths to rationalize the slaughter of the innocent for the private gain of a few"*—anonymous

Modern mechanized warfare is a multi-billion dollar industry. The stock market is a convenient way for politicians to profiteer by passing legislation favorable to the increased demand for the products of the companies they hold stock in. Since the military contractors are paid with the taxpayers' money, the people subsidize lucrative contracts, awarded by the State, to the corporations who most funded its political campaigns. An increase in profit margin for the state-assisted monopolies comes at the expense of great atrocities to the environment and the most immoral, inhumane acts in history. Not all of this money comes from tax revenue; it comes from bank loans, so people pay for it with both inflation and taxes, and the privately owned central banks grow more powerful with every war.

This blood for money game is packaged as righteous offensive-'defense' against terrorism, communism, savages, heretics; barbarians…take your pick. It's always been about controlling resources to increase the wealth of a few. The future always looks back and says, "How horrible," while they are presently on the same course under different labels. The war makers fool the public every time because the history of war is dressed up in glory instead of its soul shattering reality.

People fall in love with the tactics and the bravery; they forget it is an affair of grown adults and children solving their problems by repeated murder. Flags determine the teams, not personal quarrels. War is for the most basic animalistic part of the brain. You can live in reason or you can perpetually fight in fear. You decide.

How many times will the poor be bamboozled into fighting other poor people for the rich? How many times will the general public blindly support military misadventures because the profiting authorities told them that there was a righteous cause? How many times can a boy cry Wolfowitz? How many times can the war party flip-flop their reasons for a war? How long can the mass media cheerleaders promote each lie before the public starts to ignore what they say?

I'm sorry if I step on the feelings of those who sincerely believe that we go to war for noble dreams of freedom etc. I would like for people to see the children dying in hospitals in Palestine, caught in the fifth generation of a war where the Israelis have illegal racially segregated "settlements" with full support of the US tax dollars. Equally, I would like you to look at pictures of Fallujah after the US dropped chemical gases on the Iraqi city. What of the unmentioned 100,000–120,000 civilians killed in Iraq? Don't hide from this in denial. Don't retreat to American Idol or Desperate house whores.

Why do people hate us? There is a simple answer, and it is not because of silly cartoons. They hate us because we starve and kill them for profit. The largest genocide in history was in the Americas. It's time to stop and think about how our foreign policy affects the rest of the world. Have we really changed so much since Manifest Destiny or did we just create craftier tactics? We are still stealing, still killing, and still masking it in self-righteous propaganda deeply tied to religious dogma. The government doesn't care about you. It is still servicing the aristocrats, and we need to wake up.

4

Education is an activity, not passive memorization

o o o o o o o o o o o o o o o o o o o o o o o o o o o o o o o o o o o

"Education is what remains after one has forgotten what one has learned in school."

—*Albert Einstein*

*"Rarely is the question asked, **is** our children learning?"*

—*George W. Bush*

Congratulations, the fact that you are reading a nonfiction book about politics already makes it safe to assume that you know how to self-educate, and it separates you from most to place you in a tiny dying minority of Americans, 'people who read.' Winston Churchill is often attributed to have said, "*The biggest argument against a Democracy was a five minute conversation with the average voter.*" That kind of statement that is both funny and sad yet scary all at the same time. When I argue with people who can not name Syria's neighboring countries, or are not aware of Iraq's prior occupation by the British, or any history of the actual Middle East, and realize that their votes count as much as mine, it makes me feel as though being informed does not matter. After all, it is much easier to ignore those who read and think and treat an election like popularity contest where by the candidates can skip over knowledgeable people and aim at the herd with advertisements and one-liners. Elections become not about ideas, but manipulation of the masses, and what better way to do that than to use fear, deception, and repetition?

We have a problem (several really) with our educational system. We are also told not to talk about politics outside of designated places, as that might actually make small changes. We really are in dire straights in regards to our common political know-how, sense of citizenship, and civic duties. As some students joke when they go to school, "I am getting my *edumication*," to infer that they feel like they are learning very little, it may be time for us to start to "re-edumicate" ourselves and those around us. People cannot know what they do not know. It is time to break the taboo on discussing politics and turn it into a duty out of basic compassion and desire for justice.

A re-edumication may sound like another bad Bushism. What I think is sad is that our president defiles his native language so much that we have the term, Bushism. It should not be funny, yet that is how we cope with it. To compare Bush to any of our forefathers is like comparing Jerry Falwell to Jesus. Our education/indoctrination for the sake of occupation system is a slow death for our society and for all the forgotten knowledge that is not being passed on to the next generations. We have grown adults who can not name who the Vice President is. You would think everyone of age would know about Dick and Bush by now. Maybe that is why they can screw us over. Our Academia has no immunities either. Students in the best schools are learning many things, but there seems to be an utter void when it comes to civic duties and citizenship. Before the war, most people regardless of their level of education, could not even find Afghanistan on a map and probably had never even heard of the place, even though our own government had been financing the Taliban there and fighting a proxy war with Russia since the 1970s. No, our kids are busy being told to read fictional stories and plays at such a lopsided rate that the real world seems absolutely neglected, and there is a reason for that.

Education as opposed to *Edumication*, is what you learn outside of the walls of school and the mind numbing TV screen. It's what you learn the hard way. It's what comes from thinking for yourself, looking at the facts around you and piecing them together for a more holistic picture. True liberty and the future of our currently failing republic depend on us. Let's climb out the Rabbit hole. But before pointing fingers outward, we must point them inward and examine our own culture with a critical eye.

5

You Are Not What You Own

○ ○

"We live in a nation of gluttonous stupor and comfortable surroundings, easily distracted by the cocktail of materialism that lines our homes. We are trained to live to work, not work to live, sacrificing love of life for love for the Almighty dollar, becoming worker bees and soldier ants, selling our souls to the demons of capitalism in exchange for the happiness and stress-free lives of yesteryear, needing pharmaceutical drugs to escape the depression of our daily lives, willingly choosing to indebt our present and future in order to possess the vast array of adult toys marketed to manipulate our emotions, wrongly thinking this or that product will reincarnate lost happiness. America is the land of plenty, where waistlines expand, stress increases, mental problems grow, work hours increase and vehicles get bigger and bigger, a land addicted to the devil's excrement, like a heroin user injecting black gold into its ever thirsty veins, becoming a violent, warmongering junkie when the perpetual case of cold turkey arises"

—*Manuel Valenzuela*

The American mass media structures their programs to push hyper consumerism. This is not consumption based on function, utility, or even pleasure. It's a form of consumerism rooted on fostered insecurities and fear.

Fear sells. It not only helps sell products, it sells ideas, in particular political platforms. Deception by way of fear-mongering has been the Bush administrations' mantra. This entire war and erosion of civil liberties has been based on lies and fear. The 'murder for profit' ideology behind our hyper capitalist state is a natural extension from our 'produce and consume at any cost' culture.

We are suffering from a disease. Offshore slavery, sweat shops, exploited labor, insider trading, and profiteering are kept afloat by a steady combination of consumerism and sticking our heads in the sand. No one cares about people; not like they care about shiny things. Our nation judges its well being by the stock market or its billionaire companies and not on the welfare of the general public, our physical and psychological well being. Humanity is under the boot of the mighty dollar because of its association with self-worth.

By mixing esteem with consumerism our culture does not just buy for function and comfort, it buys for material validation; it buys to impress and gain status. Jealous people covet the jealousy of others. Prestige is often the acquisition of envy from others. It has gone way out of control. Too many people are caught in the game of 'look at me.'

People buy books that they don't even read, just for show. People will buy a piano for their house when no one even plays. People buy to impress. They buy for status. They need 'other based' validation. Does a Rolex tell time any better than a Timex? You better run to get that LV purse! High fashion makes you a 'somebody.' **You are not what you own**. Competition centers on gaining more and more property. Sadly this takes precedent over human relationships, life, and the environment. Zealous fanatical economics has been the primary reason for such institutions as slavery and Westward expansion AKA murder, thief, and cultural genocide. Many dubious rationales were given in attempts to justify the greedy ends of the hyper-consumerists. But what gave rise to the hyper-economics? How do otherwise, reasonably-moral people, rape, enslave, and murder other people and the planet? "Production" in the national sense is nothing more than gaining control of material at any cost. So how could people become so greedy?

"Growth for the sake of growth is the ideology of the cancer cell."—Edward Abbey.[1]

Greed can steer intelligence of any level. There were American frontier men and Nazis who were nice to their families and animals. There were slave owners who were upstanding individuals in other ways, and who were highly educated and intellectual. But this anything-for-profit and comfort mentality does not

---

1.   http://www.brainyquote.com/quotes/quotes/e/edwardabbe104709.html

stem from a lack of academic intelligence; it's born from a lack of compassion and susceptibility towards an egocentric truth.

In this culture a person's self worth is all wrapped up in what they can get. Getting fancy commodities, titles, and property is what constitutes "success." Without fine things you are made to feel like a failure. Generosity and compassion are only admirable qualities if they are public and thus enhance your reputation. People will horde in millions even billions and still look for more money while others starve or live in frustration working from check to check. But if you are unhappy being forced into a society that bases your human worth on your occupation and level of consumption, then somehow you are made to feel like a failure. You don't work enough; you're not smart enough etc…

Certain 'products' have phenomenally become associated with completely fabricated notions, which tie in to a person's self esteem. For example drinking has become intertwined with masculinity. The number of beers one can consume or the amount of alcohol one can 'handle' before they get drunk is somehow a sign of manliness. Beer advertisers sandwich their commercials between all male sports like football. (Kids see these commercials) Even broken men at AA meetings will smirk and take pride in the amount of alcohol they can consume.

Part of the problem with drunk driving is that the drinker does not want to admit that they are drunk, for it is a sign of being weak, and they protest admitting that they are unable to 'handle' the amount that they drank. Just having knowledge about different brands of wine and liquor is somehow a sign of high culture. (In reality drinking tolerance just reflects high prior consumption and a large body mass including a fat one) Smoking, driving cars fast, (which aids the state with costly tickets and higher insurance rates-the fact that cars even have the ability to exceed a 100 miles an hour is a mystery) owning guns, supporting the military and sports teams, and even the way we dress are associated with roles you need to play in order to "be a man." Vicarious masculinity is a problem.

Equal examples can be said for women, jewelry being the most amazing one I can think of off the top of my head. The stones have no function outside of gaining envy from others…oh the shiny things. Why does a diamond have worth? It has no value tied to its function. A diamond gets its value from the amount of envy it produces in others. Why do they envy it? Because it is expensive! Why is it expensive? Because it is envied. Advertisers and the merchant controlled media (which is dependent on advertisers) have made the diamond symbolize love. If you get a diamond or give a diamond, they say, you are loved or you love. Hey, a diamond is just a shiny stone; it only has the power that we give it. Think of it as a waste of money instead of something to impress your peers. Don't let them tell you it is necessary to give their company a large sum of money in order to get a rock, because it proves your love for someone.

Just like drinking and smoking have nothing to do with masculinity, expensive pebbles have nothing to do with love or admiration. These are all marketing scams feeding off a foolish culture. More than this, think *of how many of the diamonds were acquired.* If you didn't know already, many diamonds come from South Africa and were mined under horrible conditions where, on an average, twenty people died per week. There are so many diamonds it is ridiculous. Their market value is inflated because of artificial scarcity by DeBeers, which has a virtual monopoly. Just because it was out of sight doesn't mean it should be out of mind. Immoral acts are still immoral acts even when they are done far away.

These are not gender specific ills, but they are quite obviously lopsided with basic observation:

If a woman will run out and drop a hundred dollars on a new outfit for her own self-esteem, which is excessively tied to appearance, then that is a form of mind control. And billions are spent on advertising to insure that a bulk of women will siphon off a daily portion of their income on cosmetics, clothing, jewelry, and fashion products, including the fashion magazines (which are essentially the same gossipy recycled articles every month). Indeed, it is almost an inevitable stress for teenage girls to at some point have a conniption about not knowing what to wear. Grown women have closets just for their shoes. We are talking about more than a dozen pairs of shoes. They don't even realize the kookiness of this because it is so wide spread that it is normal in any industrialized society to be owned by the shiny things.

Cost to human health and safety is a small price to pay when it comes to consumerism, when it comes to social acceptance. So what if smoking causes cancer, cost lives and money, contributes to litter, and waste a good portion of a person's income? Smoking is profitable. Profit is a sign of production. Isn't it a price worth paying and risking to look cool, to feel posh, or to feel a little naughty?

So why is mankind's self esteem on trial here? Why is it so fragile as to be manipulated with the ease of 30 second commercials and slick magazines? 1 out of 3 people will get a cancer; 1 out of 4 women will be raped before they die and another 19% will fend off or flee from an attempt; 1 out of 4 people are infected with depression in the US; 1 out of 2 marriages will fail…We will kill animals to make clothes and shoes and then some people will kill other people, to steal them. How did the dead [objects] gain so much power over the living (people and the rest of the eco system)? Is this a healthy society? Mentally or physically?

Let's analyze the popular indoctrination our culture puts our children through; let's look at religion. Western religions are designed to break down a person's self worth and replace it with an esteem based on obedience. This is then reinforced in the educational system. In school regurgitation will carry one farther than thinking. If a young little man or lady gets out of line then we can just dope them up with Ritalin. There are exceptional teachers, but for the most part, the school system helps to enforce sex roles, and teaches people to be able to sacrifice their enjoyment in order to do what they are told. It teaches competition and the idea of the dog eat dog world.

The best way of coping with this is to take enjoyment in doing what you are told. To be a 'good boy or good girl' is to be an obedient one. And what is school really, even college? Is it what it claims to be, or is it a process which ultimately leads to an occupation? In other words, is it that which leads to a method of making money without which a person cannot obtain the basic necessities it takes to live?

Schools are having less and less to do with 'education' and more and more to do with 'indoctrination.' School has become a stepping stone into the business world. Subjects like history and geography have been so neglected that many Americans do not know where many countries are much less anything about them or our current relations. Subjects like philosophy might not even see exposure until college, and there are many who cannot even see what they are for, much less know anything about them.

A main concern for college students today is not "What can I learn?" or "How can this knowledge enhance my life, bring me pleasure, or improve my character?" The question they have on their mind is, "How can I use this?" In other words, "How can this make me money?" How many artists or similar people have turned away from their natural talents and unique process of self-actualization because it would not pay enough as an occupation? Because land and food are owned by a few, without a certain level of wage, a person can not eat or maintain even the lowest standard of living. Money becomes the focus, because without it, you have no freedom.

They don't have much of a choice in thinking this way. Knowledge doesn't pay. It's not who you are—it is who you know. Athletes and strippers make more money than philosophy and physics teachers. A recent poll shows that 1 in 10 men use Viagra. That's far more than the number of people who have read a book in the last ten years.

A good friend of mine, Anne Mills, once pointed out to me an amazing yet casually overlooked fact; "Horoscopes take up more space in the daily news paper than the latest news in science." They are in many of the little shiny magazines, too. See, people will read the utmost garbage if it is even vaguely about themselves. The majority of people reading them do not believe in them yet they are curious what *theirs* says. Worse yet, I suppose, are the people who put stock in them, these are the same kind of people who probably also believe in things like Nostradamus and Feng Sui. Well, I guess you can't reason someone out of something they were not reasoned into. Let them buy their magic headache magnets. The news itself is more of a ratings war, via entertainment, than it is informative news. Where are America's priorities? What is this leading us to? I don't know, let's ask Rome...

6

Detrimental dichotomies and self induced filters on belief constructs

○ ○

"The urge to save humanity is almost always only a false-face for the urge to rule it."

—H.L. Mencken, **Minority Report**, *1956*

It always amazes me how people will put any degree of belief in superstitions, like not having a 13th floor on hotel buildings or choosing lucky numbers for a lottery ticket, to full blown acceptance of supernatural powers manipulating the earth. Some go as far as wondering about the effects of the positions of planets on a person's birthday. Yet if you tell someone about the very real, very historically documented incidences of government corruption, media deception, and organized crime, then it is considered wacky conspiracy theory nonsense.

Is that really so? The Iran Contra affair was a huge government conspiracy which happened in my life time. It is now public knowledge. The Gulf of Tonkin incident, which dragged us into a nine-year war with Vietnam, turns out to have been falsified information used to bolster a war.[1] This was a lie that many thinking people already knew about, but the authorities did not come clean with it until 2005, several decades too late for the two million Vietnamese killed or the 55–58k Americans who died. We know the US blew up its own boat, the USS Maine, and blamed it on the Cubans in order to start the Spanish American War. The uncountable wars with American Indians were based on deceptions. Treaties were/are openly broken without apology. There is still on-going debate, but the History Channel openly states that the American government had prior knowl-

---

1.   http://en.wikipedia.org/wiki/Gulf_of_Tonkin_Resolution

edge of the Pearl Harbor attack—and did nothing because it wanted to go to war with the East, so as to seize resources and markets, which carried over into the Korean conflict. Today we seem to have a massive conspiracy of a former high-powered lobbyist, Jack Abarmoff ripping off Native American gaming tribes and bribing congress on Israel's behalf.

We know Hitler set fire to his own building, the Reichstag, and blamed it on his political enemies in order to start his imperial escapades. We know Israel was busted in a false flag operation called the Lavon affair where they bombed Western targets in Egypt and tried to blame it on Arabs. We know Israel attack an American shot the USS Liberty during the Six Day War with LBJ's approval, and tried to blame it on Arabs, until they were forced to change their story and now shamelessly claim they attacked a US ship with unmarked planes for over 3 hours by "mistake". You can bet the farm that Israel will pull a stunt in Lebanon or Syria and the US Neocons will use their propaganda to link it to Iran, as it is all part of Israel's stated policy papers from which the PNAC documents arose. We know George Bush's grandfather Prescott Bush was financing the Nazis and his son G. H. W. Bush financed and trained the Taliban. When based on substantial evidence, why is it such a giant leap of faith to believe that the Americans were lied to about Iraq, Afghanistan, and most of all September eleventh? Many Americans do more than just reject the evidence—they reject even hearing it. "Come on. The government doesn't lie…" Frankly, I think they enjoy an excuse to channel their prejudice and hatred towards a weaker enemy. It allows them to work through a power process desperately longed for in a culture of constant insecurities and steady bombardment of invalidation.

The obscene always laugh at the truth yet continue to bow to the obscene.

"The problem with politics is that it's full of politicians," I used to say. Then I added to it, "…an apathetic public is like an apathetic gardener, as soon as no one is tending, the weeds come in from everywhere." For a republic to work, people have to participate. Before people can participate, they need access to accurate information. The empire of the United States has none of these things. The news is controlled and the media lies. People pick and defend political parties like they were sports teams.

Beware of detrimental dichotomies. The way an argument is framed can be an amazing power. Americans need to see through false paradigms such as the Left vs. the Right. Every time I criticize the Neocon Republicans I get called a 'no good commie Liberal', and every time I criticize the Neocon Democrats I get called a 'crazy Right-winger'. It is automatically assumed that if you are not on one side you must be the other. What is equally as foolish is to believe that the middle is the only other position. Whoever thought to name the terms 'the left' and 'the right' was clever because it already creates either a linear or a circular spectrum for all political views. Everything is either/or. It is all one sides' view, or the other, or a compromise between the two. Third voices go unheard. Neither party will touch issues like farm subsidy abuse, Zionism, campaign finance reform, and basically our entire foreign policy. They did not argue about *if* we should go to war, only about *how* we should go to war.

When Dyncorp was caught in sex trade rings in Bosnia,[2] what did our government do? They continued to give them money. One congresswoman, Cynthia McKinney of Georgia, who is now no longer in office, gave Rumsfeld a royal grilling on the matter,[3] but the rest of congress was disturbingly quiet as was the Main Stream Media (MSM). One must ask, "Why?" Why does no one from either party, aside from one woman, raise hell about something as sick as human trafficking and sex slavery? Why was in not major news?

Whatever happened to the story about Jeff Gannon? Here we had a guy with websites offering himself up as a gay prostitute that worked for a fake news organization,[4] Talon news. It was discovered that Talon was just a GOPUSA creation. As gossipy and scandalous as the male hooker angle was, the more interesting question to ask is how Gannon made references to classified documents involving the Plame affair and internal government memos.[5]

Does it bother anyone else that New Jersey's former governor, James McGreevey, had an Israeli national as his secret boyfriend who he had propped as his Homeland Security adviser with an $110,000 salary?[6] Yet once again, the press focused more on the 'gayness' of the situation rather than the bigger story of an Israeli national sleeping his way into a position of national security.

A more damaging detrimental dichotomy than left-vs.-right political guile is the idea that logic and emotion/imagination are somehow inverse enemies. A person needs to have both to be truly intelligent. Emotion is cast off as being synonymous with being illogical and imagination is always boxed in to mean fantasy.

2.   http://www.salon.com/news/feature/2002/08/06/dyncorp/print.html
3.   March 24th CSPAN transcript http://www.fromthewilderness.com/free/ww3/
     031505_mckinney_transrcipt.shtml
     For Audio see http://mke.indymedia.org/en/2005/03/203061.shtml
4.   http://mediamatters.org/items/200501280006
5.   http://antiwar.com/justin/?articleid=4879
6.   http://www.democracynow.org/article.pl?sid=04/08/13/1410249

Being 'emotional' is painted as a person who doesn't listen to reason and is led only by their feelings. Logic has also been unfairly portrayed as being cold and uncaring. In the realms of math and the objective, logic is the same as deductive calculation. But on moral questions, logic eventually reduces back to emotion. Why is murder wrong, well because it causes people pain and suffering, and why is that wrong? Etc...etc. Eventually you have to say, "Well, I would not want to feel that way." It is wrong to believe that the injustices in our world stem from a lack of intelligence. Bad people knowingly do wrong all the time, and even good meaning people do wrong things blindly. Some of the smartest inventors, scientists, and philosophers in history were as sexist as a person could be.

America has had great leaders like Andrew Jackson who stood up to the central banks and James Madison, the father of the Bill of Rights, who were both upstanding intelligent men, but they would not skip a beat to pop off an 'Indian.' Each era has its blind spots, from slavery, to sexism, to xenophobia, to bigotry, to polluting the planet with radioactive elements, but the eye drops come from compassion not logic. We are most intelligent about the things we care about. Without compassion and emotional intelligence, logic fades into a game of making rationalizations for ends already determined to be true based on greed, fear, and a lack of understanding. Understanding requires both logic and emotion. To understand is different than to know. You can know that X number of people died in some tragic event, but you don't understand the fullness of its wrong until you feel it. As Robert G. Ingersoll once said, "Injustice will never be eradicated until those not affected by it are as outraged as those who are." Until we feel it, we will never have enough momentum to change things.

In order to feel even a fraction of what it is like to live under a military occupation, or to have a child suffering deformities from Depleted Uranium poisoning (something the US has dumped all over Iraq) Americans have to utilize their imaginations. Einstein is famous for saying, "Imagination is more important than knowledge." I am a huge fan of reason, but we tend to reason things to death or not at all. What is clearly missing from the picture is imagination. Not enough people stop and take the time to think about other people in a genuine way, imagining their life and really being there. As the Native American saying goes, "Don't judge before you walk [a mile] in his moccasins." Or in the Anglicized version, "try to put your self in their shoes." It is a cliché but it is true. Our culture puts too much emphasis on memorizing facts and not enough in really understanding their meaning. The links between imagination and creativity, to sympathy and moral character are nearly devoid; in fact they are seen as impeding clear thinking. There is a balance, without reason then you cannot even determine what is really going on in the actual world, and without emotion none of it has any meaning.

7

False paradigm of the left and right. Welcome to the Republicrats

○ ○

"We hang the petty thieves and appoint the great ones to public office."

—Aesop

"A sect or party is an elegant incognito devised to save a man from the vexation of thinking."

—Ralph Waldo Emerson

It's crucial for people to realize that this two party system is a farce. They basically have identical foreign policies. It was amazing to see such passionate fans of Kerry, who hated Bush, when Kerry was in agreement with Bush on all the major issues. The same can be said for fans of Hillary, she votes with Bush 98% of the time. It is puzzling to see how many leftist fools can criticize the Republicans who totally deserve it, yet not turn that critical eye inward on the Democrats.

During this whole run up to the war and long after the Democrats had no spine. If the Republicans are the Chicken Hawks, then the Democrats are the Chicken shits. Aside from a handful of people[1], our spineless congress rolled over for two Patriots Acts and two wars. In the face of obvious lies and blatant profiteering, they continue to give boy George and his merry band of Zionist all the money they demand.

---

1. Kucinich, Feingold, Ron Paul, Byrd, Sanders,

Congress is up for rent, what we have here is a congress made up of lobbyists' lapdogs and a President who does not believe in evolution and cannot speak without sounding like a dry-drunk[2]. In fact every time he talks it is scary, you wonder, "how he is going to butcher the English language *this* time." The fact that he meets with foreign leaders is frightening and embarrassing.
[3]

As backwards as they are, at least the Republicans believe in their own insane version of reality. We have a bad combination of no brains and no balls. The Democrats are careerists who don't have any principles or even a clear stance. The progressive Democrats seem like a different party from Hillary, Lieberman, and Kerry. But you can count the progressives with your fingers. The Democratic Party (meaning those actually in office) as a whole are trash, supported merely by those who assume that because it has a different name that it actually opposes Bush on the issues. When in reality, they agree on everything of importance. Many people who call themselves Democrats actually are opposed to the Bush administrations' policies, yet by and large the Democrats they support and have elected do not. "The party is as the party does," thus the Democrats are Neocons too. It is just like people who are conservatives, supposedly standing for less government and fiscal responsibility, voting for Neoconservatives just because they call themselves Republicans. Less government and fiscal responsibility were core conservative principles and now we have neither. The government is larger than it has ever been and we are in greater debt than we have ever been across the board on the federal and state levels. Yet people treat political parties like a favorite sports team or a religion, their party can do no wrong even when it does the very same things that are criticized when the other party does them.

One of the most wide spread complaints about pro-war Kerry was that nobody knew what he stood for. This is because Kerry was Bush-lite. The public desperately wanted an anti-Bush and were psychologically unable to understand what Kerry stood for, because him agreeing with Bush (which is what he did) didn't fit with their wishes and confused them. What we ended up with was two homophobic, pro-war, pro-Patriot Act, PNAC supporting Zionist HypoChristian fools, each trying to up the other on the religion card running for president. They both pushed the feel good macho-ism of hunting down the evil ones, by bombing countries that had nothing to do with 9/11.

---

2.   http://www.minnesotarecovery.info/literature/drydrunk.htm
3.   http://news.bbc.co.uk/1/hi/world/asia-pacific/4454738.stm

The two parties are similar to old blue jeans—different names and brands all over the world, but essentially the same thing—jeans. Their deception is as universal as white socks. In Britain they have Labor and the Conservative parties. Blair is no different than Thatcher and his other Conservative predecessors. Gordon Brown, his probable replacement, is no different than Blair himself. In Japan they are less fake about it, they really only have one party, the LDP, and it has been in charge for 53 of the last 54 years. The JPD, the next largest party, is no different though. Prime Minister Koizumi is a Neocon like Bush and Blair; he even worships at the shrines of war criminals. Fortunately Japan is limited by contract not to engage in pre-emptive war. America is the largest problem because they have the most guns and the largest market influence. So whereas I criticize the US, don't let that create the illusion that other nations are less corrupt. They are merely less corrupt because they are smaller.

The Democrats can do WAY better than Hillary Clinton—I would probably even vote for another Bush over her, and you know how I regard him. I'm not going to vote for anyone simply because she is a woman. If Hillary were a man she would have no shot. Being a woman and having a well-known last name, unfortunately, is the only thing she has going for her. She is truly terrible on every issue.

She agrees with the Neocons on everything. She is a Zionist just like Bush. She was all for the war with Afghanistan and Iraq, and she is all for a war with Iran and increasing the powers of the Patriot Act. Incidentally, she voted for them both. Don't let the media dictate your choice. By having Fox bash on Hillary, they automatically set the idea in your head that she is the next running mate. That is who they WANT to face. Is that impossible to conceive? Hillary is a Neocon, and they win either way. She is a weak candidate and no progressive could support her, just like we could not support Kerry. No one voted for Kerry. They voted against Bush.

This "let's appeal to the middle" strategy is a flop. People are dying for an actual 'Liberal' voice, an anti-war voice. Over half of the country is anti-war, but not even 2% of our congress is. So much for representative government. Please don't let the talking heads convince you that she is your only choice. They are bashing the person who they want to run against. They tremble in fear of an actual anti-war Democrat who would have a majority of the country behind him/her. Don't let this be another race between two pro-war candidates like it was for Kerry and Bush. She voted YES on loosening restrictions on cell phone wiretapping. She urged the president to veto UN condemnation of Israel. She Voted YES on $86.5 billion for military operations in Iraq & Afghanistan. She voted

YES on authorizing use of military force against Iraq. She is clearly for a war with Iran, right in step with PNAC's plans. In fact, she accused Bush of being too soft on Iran. Speaking at Princeton University she said:

"I believe that we lost critical time in dealing with Iran because the White House chose to downplay the threats and to outsource the negotiations. I don't believe you face threats like Iran or North Korea by outsourcing it to others and standing on the sidelines. But let's be clear about the threat we face now: A nuclear Iran is a danger to Israel, to its neighbors and beyond. The regime's pro-terrorist, anti-American and anti-Israel rhetoric only underscores the urgency of the threat it poses. U.S. policy must be clear and unequivocal. We cannot and should not—must not—permit Iran to build or acquire nuclear weapons. In order to prevent that from occurring, we must have more support vigorously and publicly expressed by China and Russia, and we must move as quickly as feasible for sanctions in the United Nations. And we cannot take any option off the table in sending a clear message to the current leadership of Iran—that they will not be permitted to acquire nuclear weapons."[4]

The push for Iran is centered on more lies and scare tactics, just like the build up to the war with Iraq. We have no EVIDENCE[5] of Iran building a nuclear bomb. What Iran *is* building is a pipeline to India. The true reasons for an attack on Iran are twofold. Israel says "jump" and the US says "off of what", that is the prime reason for the Zionist Neocons, but others have another more common reason and that would be the economic one. William Clarke put it like this:

"In 2005–2006, The Tehran government developed a plan to begin competing with New York's NYMEX and London's IPE with respect to international oil trades—using a euro-denominated international oil-trading mechanism. This means that without some form of US intervention, the euro is going to establish a firm foothold in the international oil trade. Given U.S. debt levels and the stated neoconservative project for U.S. global domination, Tehran's objective constitutes an obvious encroachment on U.S. dollar supremacy in the international oil market"[6]

---

4.   http://www.dailyprincetonian.com/archives/2006/01/18/news/
     14289.shtml#continue 22d paragraph
5.   http://www.washingtonpost.com/wp-dyn/content/article/2005/08/01/
     AR2005080101453.html
6.   http://www.globalresearch.ca/articles/CLA410A.html

Israel got a nice Christmas present from the US, a 600 million dollar one for 'defence.' Israel woke up Dec 25th with 600 million in aid from the US.[7] Now how much money was given to any of America's own 50 states? Louisiana, Mississippi, Alabama, Texas nor the Carolinas received that much money, even after multiple hurricanes.

Hillary supports the apartheid Wall that Israel is building across the Green Line into Palestine in order to separate a large portion of Palestine by sandwiching it between the wall and Israel proper. Israeli settlements, which would be more accurately named racially segregated Jewish colonies, are against international law. They are illegal yet Hillary supports the wall, which they call a security fence, and the accompanying forceful land grabs which consist of murder, theft, and displacement of dirt poor civilians.

"US Senator Hillary Clinton said on Sunday that she supports the separation fence Israel is building along the edges of the West Bank, and that the onus is on the Palestinian Authority to fight terrorism." [8]

This soccer mom has more of a bee in her bonnet about violent video games than she does about the Israelis doing **real** killings in Palestine. She, together with a fellow Neocon Democrat, Joe Lieberman, issued the *Family Entertainment Protection Act.*[9]

Protecting families? From video games! Oh but killing families, in the real world, is fine as long as the people being killed are enemies of the Zionists, including small children. In regards to a game called Grand Theft Auto III, she said:

"We need to do better. We need to do everything we can to make sure that parents have a line of defense against violent and graphic video games and other content that go against the values they are trying to instill in their children."[10]

---

7.   http://www.aljazeera.com/cgi-bin/news_service/
     middle_east_full_story.asp?service_id=10401
8.   http://www.dailytimes.com.pk/
     default.asp?page=2005%5C11%5C15%5Cstory_15-11-2005_pg7_53
9.   http://en.wikipedia.org/wiki/Family_Entertainment_Protection_Act
10. 7th paragraph last line.
     http://www.clinton.senate.gov/news/statements/details.cfm?id=240603&&

This woman is pro-war, pro-Zionism (aka it's not terrorism when WE do it) pro mal-corporatism, seeing as the occupation acts as a cash-cow for dirty business, and she is being touted as the Democrats next hope for president. David Swanson put it well, when he wrote in the <u>American Chronicle</u>:

"Behind curtain number one is Hillary Clinton, a pro-war, pro-CAFTA, pro-corporate health care Republicrat who is so very much more aggravating than most of them because of the widespread pretense that she's some sort of leftist or democrat with a small d."[11]

He even used the word 'Republicrat,' which I could not agree with more. The article continues, contrasting another candidate, Jonathan Tasini, with Hillary by giving him the following description:

"Behind curtain number two is Jonathan Tasini, a veteran labor organizer and strategist who opposes the war, opposes corporate trade deals, proposes to expand Medicare to universal coverage, and can be counted on to fight for working people."[12]

For the record, Tasini actually lived in Israel and has had relatives killed. He is against the Zionist occupation and supports a two-state solution.

"My father was born in Palestine and fought in the Israeli underground. I lived in Israel for seven years, during which I was involved, as a teen-ager and young man, in the fledgling peace movement. I went through the 1973 Yom Kippur war—a cousin was killed in the war and his brother was wounded. Half my family lives there, some within a few miles of the West Bank border.
So, it is absolutely clear to me that only a two-state solution will end the violence that has taken so many Palestinian and Israeli lives—and bring stability and peace to the Middle East.
I unequivocally support the creation of a Palestinian state in the West Bank and all of the Gaza Strip, consequently ending Israeli occupation of these areas because such a solution is the only way to ensure Israeli security. The final peace settlement has to accommodate Israel's security requirements but it also has to ensure a viable, thriving, independent Palestinian State which has territorial contiguity and is not broken into cantons."[13]

---

11. *http://www.americanchronicle.com/articles/viewArticle.asp?articleID=3992*
12. http://www.americanchronicle.com/articles/viewArticle.asp?articleID=3992

I like how he added, "…*which has territorial continuity and is not broken into cantons.*" This is an obvious reference to the myth of the "generous offer," which was proposed by former Prime Minister Ehud Barak. When Hillary's husband was president, it was rejected because it was anything but a generous offer. Yet they slant the language to say that they were offering a majority of the land back to Palestine. Neglected in this rhetoric is how Barak wanted to keep 69 (illegal) Settlements across the Green Line and added the provision that Palestinian land that would remain under Israeli military and civil control for an indefinite time.[14]

Did you know Bush and Kerry are relatives? Interesting how the Main Stream Media could not agree on this. MSNBC says they are 16th cousins[15]. CBS says they are 9th cousins[16].

Lewis Libby, who changed his name from Liebowitz, was the lawyer[17] from 1985 to 2000 for the criminal Marc Rich, who Bill Clinton pardoned in his 11th hour. He literally made his pardons in his last hour of his presidency. For those who don't know Libby is one of the snakes involved in the Niger forgeries and Valerie Plame investigation, more of which will be covered later. Furthermore, Lewis Libby was Richard Cheney's chief of staff, before he was indicted and forced to resign.

Marc Rich was on Interpol's Ten Most Wanted list. He smuggled oil out of Iran to Israel while the US had an embargo against Iran during the hostage crisis. He made millions selling the oil and skipped out on not paying 48 million worth on just taxes alone. That is just what he was indicted for; his true crimes were far worse, many of them perverse and tied to Mafioso in Russia[18] in particular oil and aluminum trades. He gave enormous amounts of money to both of the Clintons.

"The Rich pardon has received special attention because Denise Rich raised and donated more than $1 million to the Democratic Party in recent years and also provided the Clintons directly with a $10,000 contribution to their legal defense fund and $7,300 worth of furniture." [19]

---

13. http://www.tasinifornewyork.org/node/40
14. http://www.mediamonitors.net/gushshalom1.html
15. http://msnbc.msn.com/id/4286105/
16. http://www.cbsnews.com/stories/2004/03/04/politics/main604163.shtml
17. http://en.wikipedia.org/wiki/Lewis_Libby
18. http://www.newsmax.com/archives/articles/2001/2/16/114715.shtml
19. http://www.worldnetdaily.com/news/article.asp?ARTICLE_ID=21595 *paragraph 4*

Political parties do not matter only criminality does. In fact, hypocrisy, lying, and corruption could act as synonyms for the word 'politician' as they fit all too well with an overwhelming number of them.

Americans know that we have a locked one party system of plutocrats under two titles. Over half of the country is against the Iraq War even with the entire media and government cheerleading it. So where is **THAT** represented in our supposedly representative government? Face it; there is no Opposition Party, especially on foreign policy. The Democrats are ducking their share of the blame. What careerist cowards! No-one made the war an issue in the election. With all their millions of dollars the Democrats backed another pro-war Neocon to win the primaries and lost the election. And it appears that they are planning on doing that again with Hillary.

'Chicken Hawks' and 'Chicken Shits', that is what we have. It is a bunch of Republicrats. The Greens and Libertarians got the brains and balls but no money. Screw the Republicrats. The Democrats have failed, (except for about 7 people). Vote against every incumbent next congressional election. Show the chicken shits that they need to stand up to the Cons or they are going to be out of office.

8

Our media has failed US

○ ○
"I fear three newspapers more than a hundred thousand bayonets."

—*Napoleon*

I remember the first day of Shock and Awe. I have it all on VHS tapes. It was a sick slap in the face to listen to Wolf Blitzer of CNN pacing around panting with excitement, announcing a play by play of which oil fields we had 'liberated'. He must have said 'Shock and Awe' 50 times. In fact, my brother called me on S&A day and joked about making a drinking game out of every time the talking heads said shock and awe. They were like jubilant kids; they could not even prevent their smirking.

Prior to the war, the British had been told that within 45 minutes Saddam could spray them with chemical weapons from drone war planes. Talk about projection…When you look at these lies today, it is so clear. I used to wear a home-made T-shirt to my college that said there were no WMD in Iraq. Now some of the people, who so passionately argued against me, want to know how I knew. It was easy to know! I don't listen to the MSM. I looked at the evidence, not the corporate news.

Bush had been calling for a war with Iraq since the beginning of his presidency. Bush was having Iraq bombed 27 days after he was sworn into office. Bush was sworn in Jan 20th and bombed Baghdad with Tony Blair's assistance on Feb 16th 2001, seven months before September 11th! It was absurd how the US-UK tried to rationalize their attack as purely 'defense'. Iraqi air-defense radar was becoming too "offensive" and apparently needed to be blown up.

""The Pentagon couldn't even come up with an excuse for the bombing raid, which left two people dead and 20 severely wounded. So they called it "a routine mis-

36

sion of self defense." Their twisted logic goes this way: Because the U.S. and Britain have unilaterally declared two-thirds of Iraq to be a "no-fly zone," meaning that only they can fly there, and because the Iraqis respond to their constant over-flights with anti-aircraft fire, these two imperialist powers have the right to bomb the largest city in the country."[1]

People have no memories. Living in a world where everything CNN says is true is just unimaginable to me. In fact, truthfully, the only reason to watch the news is to gauge in which direction the propaganda is taking us and to see what they are planning,

The public is so hopelessly uninformed. There are still people who think Iraq had Weapons of Mass Destruction or that they had ties to September 11th. Some people moved on to the totally insincere rationalization of avenging the Kurds Saddam gassed in a civil war, with gas he got from the American government. Indeed, that last part is always left out. I say it is insincere because these people had never heard of the Kurds and didn't make a peep of resistance about it while it was happening. They were silent for 12 years between the event and the second Iraq war. They also did not seem to care what so ever when the US helped Turkey kill 10 times as many Kurds in 1997. [2]

The slogan for this war was "Support Our Troops". The focus of course is on the actual soldiers and not on what they are doing or if it was right. It is automatically right because to say otherwise is somehow against them. The famous linguist, Noam Chomsky, said how it was a meaningless phrase. He put it best:

"The point of public relations slogans like "Support our troops" is that they don't mean anything…That's the whole point of good propaganda. You want to create a slogan that nobody's going to be against, and everybody's going to be for. Nobody knows what it means, because it doesn't mean anything. Its crucial value is that it diverts your attention from a question that does mean something: Do you support our policy? That's the one you're not allowed to talk about."[3]—Noam Chomsky

That's just the point. Support the troops can mean supporting them in the war or supporting them by having them home. That is why it is a meaningless slogan. Imagine saying it about other wars, such as when the troops were out

---

1.   http://www.workers.org/ww/2001/iraq0301.php
2.   http://www.ratmanfrommyspace.com/1a/Noam_Chomsky_2001_1.html
3.   http://www.chomsky.info/interviews/199201—.htm the end of paragraph 8 and all of paragraph 9

West killing Native Americans. I would not support what they were doing. But I would support them in the sense that they are usually poor people fighting for the riches of another and not even knowing why they are really there. But over all I would have to cheer for the Indians, they were the ones being invaded unjustly. You can't just support the troops right or wrong. Our armies do bad things, too.

I mean obviously they are people and we don't want them killed. I have friends who are over in Iraq today. But we all know that the catch phrase "support our troops" is being used by the war party as if anyone against the war is thus against the troops too. It's 'Bushit', that is why it is a meaningless phrase.

I don't support mercenaries paid to kill strangers as a job. But I support their humanity and want them out of Iraq, and I also support the Iraqi's humanity. Because I believe, and can show how this war is a war of profiteering, I do not think that is a good enough reason for the troops to die. Nothing good has come of this war. We set up a religious theocracy and have privatized Iraq's assets to select US companies with business ties to government employees.

I think I more pity the troops than support them, because when they torture people in the prisons or when they drop chemical weapons on civilians, I can't support that. And some of them are doing that, be it out of fear, orders, or enjoyment. It is, just simply, varying degrees of wrong.

It is interesting, but I think mentally, many people with family in the military can not face the prospect that they are risking their life for nothing, for corporate expansion and the creation of a theocracy. So far in Iraq, that is all that has been done, aside from repairing things that we blew up to begin with. The war HAS to be just because they do not want to have been fooled and they do not want their sacrifices to have been in vain. Also, part of the military pride is the self-righteousness of saying they fight for freedom. When, and if they discover, they are not fighting for freedom but dying for profit margins it is too much to handle because it strips away the pride and forces them to recognize they have been pawns.

It is unpopular to say, but a large chunk of our military recruits are just poor kids who screwed up in high school. The service offers them three things they have never had: respect, an above mediocre income, and a chance at college. The largest recipient of welfare in the US is white women; the men have the military to hide in. We aren't fighting the Germans and the Japanese war machines. We are fighting out gunned, out financed, out armored, unprofessional, completely technologically inferior, desperate civilian guerillas with no air force, no navy, or heavy armor. And we are losing good young people every day in a war of attrition from an enemy that has nothing to lose and everything to gain. Remember when

Cheney and Rumsfeld said we would be greeted in the streets with flowers? I cannot tell if that is more deception or just unbelievable arrogance. These people do not live in reality; they live in the land of fantasy.

9

You can not trust the press

Remember the staged toppling of the Saddam statue? They certainly showed the statue coming down, but what they did not show was how the entrance to the park was blocked and this was a planned propaganda stunt using Chalabi and his goons as actors. It was aired in the UK, but it did not make the televised news in the US.

Here is a photo that you may have missed: [1]

The BBC had extensive coverage of this event. It is strange how well the US can blackout information, even when it is on TV overseas in the same language.

If we turn to the talking heads for all of our information without questioning their influences and motives to present a dishonest portrayal of things, if we do not exercise prudence in the wake of their past lies and fear-mongering, we are doomed. Not independently reading (books or the web) greatly reduces the kind of information one has access to and our lead by profit, celebrity chasing, sensationalist, mass media does more than not cover news. They actually champion disinformation when it overlaps with their owners' profits. Control of information is vital to any functioning republic. And make no mistake about it; we are in an information war.

The media is a keystone for all of these other ills. Books, radio and the Internet are chipping away at the information monopoly. A power shift has slowly been occurring. More and more people are sick of the lies on TV and are looking for alternative sources of information that are less polluted by economic bias or the personal ideologies of a network owner who is beholden to corporate advertising. Unplug yourself (if you have not already) from Fox News, ABCNNBCBS news and also the trash in the written press like the New York Times, which actively acted as war propaganda with Judith Miller and others.

Our mass media is an absolute joke. The 'news' has become entertainment. News networks have to compete with each other. Jerry Springer-style entertain-

---

1.   http://media.consumercide.com/saddamstatue.html

ment sells better than actual news. The average wage worker uses TV as a form of escapism and relaxation. The networks have slowly been shifting towards entertainment because that gets higher ratings than news. The talking heads on TV are vying for celebrity status. They want their own reputations as entertainers not conveyors of information. Our businesses run off of the profit motive. Importance no longer matters as much as entertainment value, thus the Scott Peterson trial has more coverage than the Enron scandal. Where are those trials? Our networks have become pundits of celebrity trash and gossip akin to fake journalistic magazines and off the wall talk shows.

No one in the mass media did their job in investigating the reports that gave us all the false pretexts[2] for going to war in Iraq. They spoon-fed us the lies by reiterating them, as if they were a mouth-piece for the president. They entice whatever propaganda is profitable as a business—such as a war—rather than trying to find out facts and doing some real journalism. They spout out talking points from a highly centralized and near monopoly of media ownership involving only a handful of men. What furthers a career in the media is not investigative journalism or accurate reports. What furthers one's career is obedience. They take their cues from the top and then try to out do each other in spinning the message. If they question something, they get replaced.

The segments where they interview people have become partisan 'hackery' contest which often drizzles down to the level of arguments on a middle school bus, complete with name calling, shouting shut up, and talking over one another.

It is only going to get worse. To keep up in ratings, each network must dumb it down, keep it shocking, and increasingly have it filled with anger and plenty of polarized issues. In an ironic paradox of being both funny, yet sad at the same time, the comedy and entertainment channels have become more reliable and better sources of news than the actual news. This role reversal is one of those things that is so deeply troubling that you have to laugh about it a little just from the disbelief.

As citizens we have a responsibility. The media is not going to reform itself. We need to turn off the TV. We need to rise above this 'panem et circenses'[3] for the 'hoi poli.'[4] We need to organize and show up outside the office buildings of televised and print media and demand a change. This is not just a problem with FOX News as many people have caught on to; CNN and MSNBC are just as far

---

2.   http://www.whatreallyhappened.com/trailofdisinformation.html
3.   bread and circuses
4.   common people (*negative connotation*)

out there as FOX. Scarborough is just as bad as O'Reilly, and I don't think anyone is as bad as, former AIPAC employee, Wolf Blitzer from CNN. These guys have turned the news into a circus.

Our congress seems just as bad. When it comes to minor things the parties bicker like Hackfields and McCoys, but when it comes to an unjust and fabricated war cry, they are uniform in their bobbing heads. They must have all drunk the same Kool-Aid when they irresponsibly passed a PATRIOT Act without even reading it. With four or five exceptions, we should not be voting for a single incumbent next election.

We, the public, have duties too. We can not sit around hoping things will change by themselves or that some leader will save us. We need to exercise our constitutional rights and go out and protest this one party America and the mass media which has fallen victim to the failings of a capitalist system's weakness to money.

Because big media is beholden to big money, there is an intrinsic bias toward profit while humanity gets crushed. The coverage of Israel's Occupation of Palestine5 or the number of civilian deaths in Iraq are the most blatant examples.

This is not a Bush thing; this is a problem with the system. All of the presidents in my lifetime have been guilty of it. Congress, the DoD and the State department were all complacent in the fear-induced war. Our problem here is a plutocracy. In the last presidential election of 2004, 96% of the time, whoever spent the most dollars won his/her race. Now when is the mainstream press going to report that?

If you want to know how important the media is to the government look at the recently revealed memo of Bush's plans to bomb Al-Jazeera in Qatar! Seriously, if they can't control the media they will destroy it. Fortunately, Tony Blair talked him out of it.

"The No. 10 memo now raises fresh doubts over US claims that previous attacks against al-Jazeera staff were military errors. In 2001 the station's Kabul office was knocked out by two "smart" bombs. In 2003, al-Jazeera reporter Tareq Ayyoub was killed in a US missile strike on the station's Baghdad centre."[5]
It took over a year for media to mention the United States used chemical weapons on the city of Fallujah in Iraq. That is terrorism, when innocents are

---

5.   http://www.mirror.co.uk/news/
      tm_objectid=16397937&method=full&siteid=94762&headline=exclusive—
      bush-plot-to-bomb-his-arab-ally-name_page.html

massacred from the skies as if by some glowing white angel of death, in a brutal indiscriminate slaughter. Justin Raimondo's words captured it best;

"The death visited by phosphorous bombs is an eerie one: the bombs explode and spread a lethal cloud that goes right through clothing and seeks out flesh, searing and eating it up like some airborne ghoul. We are confronted with the sight of charred skeletons, the skin dripping off the bone, with clothing still clinging to the corpses."[6]

At present, the American media **still** has not made any mention of it. Why? Because the media is an arm of the government so it is not going to report what is really happening. Not only has it not been reported in the US, but in two separate instances, Italian journalists who were not part of the approved embedded press were shot at, supposedly by mistake, by US troops. One of them, Giuliana Sgrena, survived.

"An Italian secret service agent, Nicola Calipari, who negotiated Ms Sgrena's release, died as he shielded Ms Sgrena from the shots."[7]

Well, thank you Nicola Calipari. Sgrena has reported what she found. And on November 8th 2005 it finally hit the airwaves but only on the web if you live in America.

It is a sick taste of irony, the kind where people were burned alive, that the US went to war with the false claims of Weapons of mass destruction and then used MK77 (upgraded napalm) and white phosphorus on a civilian population. Equally as important is the story of the media black out. It was a total cover up.

---

6. http://antiwar.com/justin/?articleid=7993 12th paragraph down.
7. http://news.bbc.co.uk/2/hi/europe/4323361.stm 4th paragraph down

10

The Embedded Media is in-bed with the Administration.

"It's no more Anti-Semitic to criticize Israel than criticizing the Nazis would be Anti-White"

—*Ryan Dawson*

Let us look at a few stories from the past year that were either spun or completely ignored. We will start by quickly outlining five huge lies the government told about Iraq. We will explore how the media was complacent, learn what really happened, and then get into the real elephant in the room, the most taboo sacred cow of them all, Israel and its much enjoyed double standards.

Claim 1
[**GOV**] There is no doubt Iraq has weapons of Mass destruction. They must disarm or there will be war. (However, Bush put it, only as our last option, 'our option of **last** resort,' This is more double speak where black is white and white is black, because war was always this administration's **first** option, a determination only.)
[**MSM**] Fox ABCNNBCBS all reiterated the government's claims that were based on no evidence but on trust. They ignored dissenting voices like the former Chief weapons inspector Scott Ritter, the (IAEA) International Atomic Energy Agency, and the combined intelligence of the entire international community.
[**Extra fact**] After Gulf War I, the deal with Iraq was that they had to disarm and comply with inspections. Sanctions were put into place that led to the starvation of thousands of Iraqi children. The sanctions were not removed when Iraq complied with the disbarment. The US kept them and upped the ante to regime

44

change, something that had never been agreed upon. Iraq was bombed daily in the "no fly zone" and constantly provoked by the US to offer a pretext for another invasion. To make matters worse the US weapons inspectors were caught acting as spies for the CIA under Clinton. That is why they were withdrawn, they were never kicked out. Not once did the televised media mention any of this.

[**Truth**] Iraq did not have any weapons of mass destruction and the so-called evidence the US was using was fabrications from Team Chalabi and Team OSP. The hunt for WMD's had now been called off but not before we wasted billions of dollars on it.[1]

[**Interesting tidbit**] Remember when Halliburton-KBR got caught overcharging and getting kickbacks in Kuwait? What were they building…?

[**ISRAEL**] Israel on the other hand does have weapons of mass destruction and they have used them. They have dropped deadly gas on parts of Palestine, killing indiscriminately.

Claim 2

[**GOV**] Iraq is trying to build a nuclear bomb and could build one within a year. *"We can not wait for the smoking gun to be a mushroom cloud."*[2] And of course you have Judith Miller's infamous zinger about the aluminum tubes being used as centrifuges. (This was pure scare tactics).

[**MSM**] The administration's talking points were blasted all over the media. It is funny how all the major networks will use the same catch phrases and report the same stories often in the same order. No-one in the media gave a voice to the atomic energy agencies which reported that Iraq had no nuclear capabilities.

[**Truth**] Iraq had no nuclear capacity. They didn't even have an air force, much less a nuclear program or material.

[**ISRAEL**] Israel on the other hand has secretly built nukes; as many as 200 nuclear weapons.[3] They still officially deny it but they are not fooling anyone. It's an open secret.[4] In the 1980s a former worker at the plant, Mordechai Vanunu, narked to the British about their operation, and showed them photographs of nuclear warheads. Israel is not subjected to routine nuclear inspections like everyone else in the nuclear club. Interestingly, they had a conniption fit when Syria called for a ban of all WMD in the Middle East. Iran and Libya opened up to inspections, but not Israel, never Israel.

---

1. And obviously we already knew the answer since we were lying it was a pay out.
2. Condoleezza Rice
3. http://news.bbc.co.uk/1/hi/world/middle_east/892941.stm
4. http://news.bbc.co.uk/2/hi/middle_east/3340639.stm

[**Interesting tidbit**] We are hearing the same propaganda about nukes with Iran, even though we have no evidence and the IAEA has said Iran is not enriching uranium for nuclear weapons. I believe it was Bush who said,

"Fool me once...er uh fool me twice...er uh well you ain't gonna fool me again."

Claim 3

[**GOV**] Saddam is acquiring uranium from Africa [Niger]. Who said it? Bush, Cheney and Condoleezza Rice, so no one important...

[**MSM**] Backed this up completely and when it finally became public that the Niger documents were determined to be forgeries, there was an eerie silence in the televised media. This should have been headline non-stop news. They were lying us into a war.

[**Interesting tidbit**] Note how little coverage was given to the world's largest protest before the war in Iraq, where Millions of people from the US to Africa to Japan protested worldwide against the war. Apparently, not everyone relies on Fox and ABCNNBCBS for their news.

[**Truth**] Iraq was not trying to acquire uranium from anyone. The administration knew this because they had invented the documents making the claims.

[**ISRAEL**] Israel has a long history of spying on the United States. The most famous failed spy, Jonathon Pollard, delivered over 1000 classified documents to Israel.

"But by far the most egregious damage done by Pollard was to steal classified documents relating to the US Nuclear Deterrent relative to the USSR and send them to Israel. According to sources in the US State Department, Israel then turned around and traded those stolen nuclear secrets to the USSR in exchange for increased emigration quotas from the USSR to Israel."[5]

[**Extra Fact**] Well, doesn't that sound familiar? The US's programs for nuclear deterrents were undermined by Israeli spies. Well, let's see what has been happening today. Valarie Plame is ousted from the CIA, revealing her front company whose agents were in charge of tracking nuclear weapons proliferation. Concurrently, we have AIPAC, Israel's largest lobby group, being busted by the FBI for spying on the United States while handing over top secret documents to Israel by Larry Franklin who worked in the DOD for the Office of Special Plans. This was

---

5.   http://www.whatreallyhappened.com/motherofallscandals.html

the same group involved in the Niger forgeries, who falsely accused Iraq of build-ing Nuclear weapons. One of his bosses was Richard Perle, who got caught in the 1970s spying for Israel then just so happened to decide to resign. When Perle was working for Senator Henry Swoop Jackson and gave classified information to Israel, not a thing was done about it.[6] Now why would that be?

"Further controversy followed in 1970. An FBI wiretap authorized for the Israeli Embassy picked up Perle discussing with an Embassy official classified information which he said had been supplied to by a staff member on the National Security Coun-cil. From 1981 to 1987, Perle was Assistant Secretary of Defense for international security policy in the Reagan administration. Perle was widely criticized after it was reported that he had recommended that the Army purchase an armaments system from an Israeli company that a year earlier had paid him $50,000 in consulting fees."[7]

Along with Perle, was his deputy Douglas Feith, who also decided it was a good time to resign. Perle was chairman of the Defense Policy Board and Feith was undersecretary of defense for policy. Perle, who has the nick name 'Prince of Darkness', was also a principle author of PNAC. This guy has absolutely no redeeming qualities and is deserving of a fate, equally as dismal as Ariel Sharon's. [**Some interesting History**] In 1954 Israel acted out a false flag operation called the Lavon Affair also known as Operation Suzannah, where Egyptian Jews and undercover Israeli agents ran around Egypt bombing western targets and then tried to blame it on Arabs.

"Egyptian authorities arrested one suspect, Robert Dassa, when his bomb accidentally ignited prematurely in his pocket. Having searched his apartment, they found incrim-inating evidence and names of accomplices to the operation. Several suspects were arrested, including Egyptian Jews and undercover Israelis."[8]

Claim 4
[**GOV**] Saddam killed his own people. Saddam gassed the Kurds 12 years ago.
[**MEDIA**] Wait, didn't I just write what the media said? Oh, that was the govern-ment. Same difference! What the media did not mention was that the US gave Saddam the gas he used on the Kurds, which was during a Civil War/War with

---

6.
7.   http://en.wikipedia.org/wiki/Richard_Perle
8.   http://en.wikipedia.org/wiki/Lavon_Affair

Iran. In fact, Secretary Rumsfeld was the fool making the deal, and Dow Chemical sold 1.5million dollars worth of pesticides which easily double as chemical weapons. Now, that is part of the story we didn't see in the media.

[**Truth**] Saddam was a bastard and America was assisting him when he committed these horrible acts—much like how the US government aided and trained the Taliban in Afghanistan.

[**Israel**] No one kills civilians like Israel. It is the only country on earth with open ethnic cleansing to set up neighborhoods and cities for a self proclaimed chosen race. Har'rats and the Jerusalem Post, both Israeli papers, have broken the stories of how Israel has even attacked its own people in fake Al Qaeda operations!

Claim 5

[**GOV**] Iraq is breaking UN resolutions. In particular UN resolution 1441 which said they could not possess WMD. (Turns out they were complying with that one)

[**MEDIA**] Basically the media were parroting what the government said. dissenting voices were silenced and the government's in-house clean up went virtually unreported. At no point did it mention how US sanctions had been starving thousands of Iraqis for 12 years. No, *that's* not a crime. Americans killed far more Iraqis than Saddam.

[**Truth**] The US government was lying about its claims.

[**ISRAEL**] Right now Israel holds the record for breaking the most UN resolutions. In fact they are breaking more by themselves than all other countries put together. Israel is currently breaking 60 different UN resolutions and has voted solo with the US veto power against every other nation countless times.[9]

"Israel has violated more that 60 UN Security Council resolutions and has never recognized the constraints of UNR 242 and 338 which requires the relinquishing of the parts of Palestine taken by force in the '67 War, much less UN Resolution 194 which call for the reparation of the indigenous Palestinian population expelled from Palestine in 1948."[10]

9.   http://www.jewishvirtuallibrary.org/jsource/UN/usvetoes.html
10.   http://counterpunch.org/martin07012004.html

11

More media lies and media censorship

"Any dictator would admire the uniformity and obedience of the US media"

—*Noam Chomsky*

The liars and suppliers (*suppliars* you could call them) were not isolated to just Iraq. The press calls it *spin*, but let's just call it what it is, spin is a more acceptable word for lying. The mainstream media lies about basically everything. For example, during the London bombings on July 7th 2005, the catch phrase became, "We shall hold our resolve."

It is amazing how all the networks will say the same things, with the same catch phrases and have the same stories often in the same order.

The propaganda package was set in place ready to roll before the attacks occurred—immediately after the Neocons said that Spain caved in to the terrorists on the 3/11 Madrid bombings, because they left Iraq after a horrific train bombing. First of all, Spain was pulling out of the war anyway. The new president had run on an anti-war ticket from the start and, according to polls, an overwhelming majority of Spain did not want the war and never did. Saying that Spain pulled out of the Iraq War, because of the train bombings, was obvious US media propaganda. It can be looked up; José Luis Rodriguez Zapatero was against the Iraq war from the beginning. Secondly, for the one millionth time, Iraq is NOT Al Qaeda! So, pulling out of the Iraq War would actually allow Spain to have more troops and money to fight actual terrorists.

Now how does this relate to the bombing in London you may ask?

Well, the American media was linking the attacks to Iraq within the first hour. They started to say all of the above mentioned BS about Spain. Then, they shot off some more rhetoric about 9/11 (which also had nothing to do with Iraq). In this, they linked the concept of maintaining support for the war in Iraq, while showing that the British were "holding their resolve" against the terrorists. If they didn't support the war in Iraq then they were caving into the terrorists, the way Spain supposedly did.

Now, why did the attack in London happen anyway, and why are there terrorists? Whose interests did it serve? IF, and I mean a big IF it were actual terrorists and not a government orchestrated distraction from the DSMs (Downing Street Memos) and Plame scandals, then it seems timely to come at the foot of the G8 Summit, which was converted into a war on terror meeting.

The spin with Spain and the smear is so clear. All one has to do is go read about the Spanish election prior to 3/11, and it is quite obvious they wanted out of the war and Zapatero ran on an anti-war ticket. That is what democratic republics do; they obey the will of the people so long as it is in accordance with their respective constitution. Also, the former president tried to link the train bombing to the ETA, which proved to be false, and that turned off the public.

How many people know that AIPAC, the largest Israeli lobby group in the US, has been caught red handed in a spy scandal? The TV news has not dared mention it, but Larry Franklin, a mid-level pentagon trader, has pleaded guilty to handing top secret US documents to Israel using AIPAC officials Keith Wiessman and Steven Rosen as the handlers. Both of the AIPAC officials have been fired. They actually have the gall to sue too; they are suing AIPAC since (they say) it knew full well what they were doing and approved of it. No, the news was busy with Michael Jackson at the time. It's kind of like how obsessed they became with Lacy Peterson at a time when the US was caught systematically torturing prisoners—and even taking photos of it—in Abu Ghraib! And to this day only the surface of those horrid images have made their way to the public.

There are reports of people wrapped in Israeli flags being made to roll in broken glass to create human tampons. People with forced feeding tubes in all their orifices inducing them to vomit; when asked about that Rumsfeld said, I am not a doctor. People stripped naked and attacked by trained dogs…people stripped and left to freeze outside in the desert night…people electrocuted, having their joints drilled, being hog tied for 20 hour periods, people being sodomized, people having their loved ones dragged out in front of them and raped including their children, people being left inside clear plastic coffins to watch one another suffocate to death in the back of trucks. Oh, these things cannot be true, can they?

The press/government would have us believe the known torturers who were stupid enough (and apparently unafraid enough) to take pictures and make films of what they were doing, were just a few bad apples. I wish I could believe that. But we have Brig. Gen. Janis Karpinski, former commander of the 800th Military Police Brigade at Abu Ghraib speaking, out saying that CIA interrogators work in special cell blocks torturing prisoners.

"American Civil Liberties Union has released new documents this week that indicate at least 21 detainees have been murdered at U.S. facilities in Iraq and Afghanistan. The ACLU came to the conclusion after obtaining reams of released Pentagon documents. According to the group, the documents show that detainees were hooded, gagged, strangled, beaten with blunt objects, subjected to sleep deprivation and to hot and cold environmental conditions"[1]

Keep in mind these are not terrorists, they are fighters in Iraq. Sure, some of them attack the US military but that is what the opposing force does in a war. Iraq had absolutely nothing to do with 9/11. Furthermore, returning soldiers have returned home saying many of the people are arrested along with the insurgents. In fact, the majority of the prisoners came from random sweeps, where all males of a certain age group in a given area are arrested or they were there for petty crimes.

Aidan Delgado,[2] who spent six months helping run Abu Ghraib, has a shocking story. This honorable young man had an epiphany he attributes to his religion (Buddhism) while on his tour of duty. He was looking around at the people they were fighting and witnessing the abuse some American soldiers were inflicting on the local Iraqis which was normally racially motivated, and he thought to himself, my enemy is just like us, they are often poor young men.

He was at Abu Ghraib when five unarmed prisoners were shot. One was shot in the groin with a machine gun and took three days to die. Photos of the event were posted and bragged about by his command. Hear his story for yourself.[3]

Of course, you are not allowed to show the US in a bad light even if it is true. You get fired from your job if you so much as release pictures of US flag draped coffins.[4] It pops the 'see no evil' bubble. You can show dead people from the tsunami, you can show dead people in Iraq, but do not show funerals for the US.

1.   http://www.democracynow.org/article.pl?sid=05/10/26/1423248
2.   http://www.informationclearinghouse.info/article8441.htm
3.   http://www.informationclearinghouse.info/article7508.htm
4.   http://www.chinadaily.com.cn/english/doc/2004-04/24/content_325966.htm

12

What we don't know can be Torturous.

○ ○

"No person under any form of detention or imprisonment shall be subjected to torture or to cruel, inhuman or degrading treatment or punishment. No circumstance whatever may be invoked as a justification for torture or other cruel, inhuman or degrading treatment or punishment."[1]

—Adopted by the UN General Assembly resolution 43/173[2] *of 9 December 1988*

When I was a child, I never thought that there would ever come a day when there would ever be a need for what I am about to do. It is a very sad state of humanity when someone even has to entertain the thought of explaining why such a hideous thing like torture is wrong. One would assume that this was fairly self-evident. Torture may very well be the most horrible action any human being could possibly do to another human being.

In Guantanamo Bay, US military interrogators have sank to a level of savagery consisting of conventional beatings and physicality like hog-tying people for 24 hour periods, to rather unorthodox and psychological methods of interrogation whereby a prisoner's religious taboos regarding sexuality are used against them.

---

1. http://www.unhchr.ch/html/menu3/b/h_comp36.htm Principle 6 ~ Body of Principles for the Protection of All Persons under Any Form of Detention or Imprisonment. Adopted by General Assembly resolution 43/173 of 9 December 1988.

2. http://www.un.org/documents/ga/res/43/a43r173.htm

On CBS's May 1st addition of 60 minutes, Sgt. Erik Saar, a former translator at Guantanamo Bay, explained that the bizarre methods, whereby prisoners had been subjected to sacrilegious sexual situations, such as being touched by menstrual blood and tantalized in various improper ways, was used so often that there was a term for it. 'Sexed up' was slang for these rather purposeless acts of mental torment in the prison.

Where as the 'Sexed Up' method of torment may entice more of a public interest by its unusual nature, it must be remembered that the physical beatings are far more grotesque and against international law and American values. The MSM press cleverly made a huge focus on an alleged desecration of the Koran. They ran stories for three days about a Koran (possibly) being flushed down a toilet. What this did was undermine the talk about torture, spinning it as though the worst of what went on was the psychological torment of defiling a person's religion. When Afghanistan had an upstart about the revelations of the torture, the media made it appear to be all about religion and flushing a book down a toilet or guards urinating on some pages. Not that those things are insignificant, but they were absolutely minor relative to the other crimes.

The Danish cartoons fiasco is a repeat of this tactic. Bush is in hot water for the NSA's SS-like spying and has again set a fire in the Middle East by stating his desire to cut aid to the democratically elected party of Hamas in Palestine. Why is it that cartoons get more press then actual crimes like the chemical bombing of Fallujah? It is just the breaking point. Like the LA riots of 1992 had little to do with Rodney King or race relations. It was about the long standing corruption of the police and court systems. The Middle East has half a million reasons to be irate at the West. More Abu Ghraib photos have been released[3] with perfect timing, overlapping with the so called cartoon fall out; to further insure continued mayhem in the Middle East. What other than perhaps genocide could be worse than systematic and sadist torture? From Iraq to Cuba the US is engaged in utterly disgusting and unnecessary torturous crimes which often have a sexual undertone. It should turn your stomach just to know about these things.

Army Col. Patrick Lang (of Gitmo) expressed how ashamed it made him feel to think that the US had stooped to such a disgraceful low:

"As a professional soldier, and someone who dedicated his life to the service of the United States, in fact, to think that United States would stoop to such tactics as this, I find to be a disgraceful thing."[4]

---

3.   http://www.uruknet.info/?p=m20640&l=i&size=1&hd=0

The guilt, or at least, the intellectual acknowledgment by the perpetrators that the prison fiasco in which these Guantanamo Bay interrogators were engaged in, was wrong, illegal, or at least not politically acceptable, can be deduced from the attempted cover up. They knew what they were doing was illegal and immoral. They knew it was not even helpful and did not work as a useful interrogation method. When bigwigs came to visit Gitmo the sadistic monsters faked some more evidence.

"Authorities at Guantanamo Bay staged interrogations of detainees for visiting politicians and generals to give the impression that valuable intelligence was regularly being gathered, says a former US Army translator at the camp. Sergeant Erik Saar told CBS television's 60 Minutes that he believed "only a few dozen" of the 600 detainees at the camp were terrorists and that little information was obtained from them." [5]

If the US is staging fake interrogations for VIPs, then it is admitting that it knows that no usable intelligence is being gathered from torturing the prisoners. They must be fully aware that what they are doing is wrong or else they would not be trying to hide it or rationalize it. So why are they torturing them? Well, for the same reason they dumped chemical weapons on Fallujah (in operation phantom fury) after a war they had already declared they had won. These people actually get off on it.

It is interesting to note that Lewis Libby was Marc Rich's lawyer a man involved in everything from tax fraud to illegal oil trades and the infamous looting scam of the "privatization" of Russia during the collapse of the Soviet Union. Then we have Libby writing fictional books with an underage Japanese girl being raped by a bear.[6] Tie all of that in with Jeff Gannon a homosexual male prostitute working for a fake news agency (talon news) and having access to the highest levels of the White House. Mary Kate Letourneau, remember the woman who went to jail for the statutory rape of one of her sixth grade students and got pregnant from it?[7] Well her brother is Joseph E. Schmitz Pentagon's former inspector gen-

---

4.   http://www.cbsnews.com/stories/2005/04/28/60minutes/
      main691602_page3.shtml
5.   http://www.theaustralian.news.com.au/common/story_page/
      0,5744,15122310%255E1702,00.html
6.   http://www.newyorker.com/talk/content/articles/051107ta_talk_collins
7.   http://www.courttv.com/archive/casefiles/verdicts/letourneau.html

eral who now works for the Prince Group[8] the parent company for Blackwater USA which is a company that spits out private contractors to help with 'security' in Iraq. And we all know how that went. Then we got Neil Bush, George W's brother, caught up in a scandal involving prostitutes in South East Asia…What is wrong with these people?

This is not something new. The US has been caught torturing before. We all heard about Abu Ghraib in Iraq, which was sickening and bad enough by its self. However, the US has also been involved in what can be called **'torture by proxy.'** The US simply has "renditions": where prisoners are taken to countries where torture is legal or can be done with authorities looking the other way. As late as November of 2004 the British news paper The Sunday Times reported of an executive jet, being used by the American intelligence agencies to fly terrorist suspects to countries that routinely use torture in their prisons

"*The movements of the Gulfstream 5 leased by agents from the United States defense department and the CIA are detailed in confidential logs obtained by The Sunday Times which cover more than 300 flights.*

Countries with poor human rights records to which the Americans have delivered prisoners include Egypt, Syria and Uzbekistan, according to the files. The logs have prompted allegations from critics that the agency is using such regimes to carry out 'torture by proxy' 'a charge denied by the American government."[9]

To add to this appalling new low of American practices is the venom being spewed by the Neo-Con variety of talking heads who actually have the audacity after failed attempts at denial and a cover-up, to try to justify the use of torture. The wild scenario of torture being needed to extract information from someone to save people from some impending doom just isn't real.

Torture is not effective, more often you get what you want to hear and not what is true. We know for a fact that any torture that lead to information about Saddam's mythical WMDs had to be false, because you can't know about something that does not really exist. Even if torture were an effective method it would not matter because it is plainly immoral and inhumane.

If the police are chasing a robber in the streets, they could in theory whip out a bazooka and blow the suspect away along with a quarter of a city block and

---

8.   http://www.washingtonpost.com/wp-dyn/content/article/2005/08/31/
      AR2005083102602.html
9.   http://www.timesonline.co.uk/article/0,2089-1357699,00.html

innocent people. The criminal would indeed be stopped, but at what price? Any civilians killed and all the destruction of property would be colored in military language as "collateral damage."

These interrogators are sick individuals who are aiming more at getting off their jollies and relieving stress than obtaining valuable information. In Abu Ghraib some of the guards were having contests, before the brashness of taking pictures and the documentation of the sadistic things they were doing was finally leaked by an upstanding honest soldier, Joe Darby. Military intelligence interrogators also told investigators that two dog handlers at Abu Ghraib were "having a contest" to see how many detainees they could make involuntarily urinate, from fear of the dogs, according to the previously undisclosed statements obtained by The Washington Post.[10]

Deborah Davies, a reporter for Channel 4 Dispatches, explains while talking about prisoners, 'that they were just some of the victims of wholesale torture taking place inside the U.S. prison system that we uncovered during a four-month investigation for BBC Channel 4'. It' is terrible to watch some of the videos and realize that you're not only seeing torture in action but, in the most extreme cases, you are witnessing young men dying.

The prison guards stand over their captives with electric cattle prods, stun guns, and dogs. Many of the prisoners have been ordered to strip naked. The guards are yelling abuse at them, ordering them to lie on the ground and crawl. On the Channel 4 documentary the guards can be plainly heard shouting with delight at the nude prisoners who are worming on the ground, 'Crawl motherfuckers, crawl'.

If the American prison system within the US is any indication of how dehumanizing authority figures can be, or how far our moral compass has atrophied from neglected oversight and apparently, a quite costly over trust in prison administrators, then these torturous military prison camps are just extensions of a greater disease.

The head of the ACLU, Anthony Romero, had more to add, not just about the immoral aspect of torture, but also how it was not pragmatic, and actually detrimental, in the process of gathering intelligence. He said that the FBI was worried that their chance of finding out reliable information was being ruined by these highly unethical and unconstructive methods being used in Guantanamo Bay.

---

10. *By Josh White and Scott Higham* Washington Post Staff Writers Friday, June 11, 2004; Page A01 http://www.informationclearinghouse.info/article6316.htm

This part of the argument should not even be necessary. As normal, sane, functioning compassionate human beings, we should be outraged by the use of torture and the jolly little games these perpetrators have been engaged in for years, not just in military prisons, but prison systems in general. There was more of an outrage from congress about Terry Schiavo than about the widespread use of torture and killing of innocents.

Torturing prisoners of war is against the Geneva Conventions. The US simply does not classify these prisoners of war, who, by and large were captured in the field of battle in Afghanistan during a war, as prisoners of war. They conveniently categorize them as 'terrorists' and by doing so they are not subject to the rules of the Geneva Conventions. Moreover, many of the men are innocent, as it has been reported that soldiers are given orders to simply arrest Iraqis at random![11]

The US's redefinition of POWs to terrorists is just another sick display of a disregard for the rules much akin to America's refusal to enforce UN resolutions in Israel, such as 242. This is more than likely because Israel is a cash-cow for the American military-industrial complex. They make laws of convenience ignoring its own agreements when it is fitting for them, just ask any Native American Indian nation how trustworthy any documented agreement is with the US when enough money is involved. At the root of this, there is a cultural problem, the disturbing obsession with money, and how any and all ethical dilemmas are tossed out the window when 'egoism' and profit are involved.

But that is not enough. Recently, we have a couple torture whammies. First congress introduces a bill that basically says we can only torture a little bit. Senator McCain who was a Vietnam POW introduced the bill. This bill should not even be necessary as it is already part of our own signed international law that torture is illegal. Well it was approved 90 to 9. Who were the sick nine senators who said no? Senator Allard (CO) Senator Bond (MO) Both Oklahoma senators Coburn and Inhofe, Senator Stevens (AK) Senator Session (AL) Senator Roberts of Kansas the state which recently implemented intelligent design fairytales over evolution and empirical evidence, and Senator Cornyn (TX) all of whom are Republicans.[12]

If you live in any of these states, vote these people out of office. Bush who has never vetoed anything said he would veto this bill and the Vice president is in full agreement. On top of all of this is the second whammy. The CIA's secret camps

---

11.   http://www.guardian.co.uk/Iraq/Story/0,2763,1211374,00.html
12.   http://www.prisonplanet.com/articles/october2005/081005perspective.htm

in Eastern Europe have been exposed and Bush wants the CIA to be exempt from torture and interrogation laws. Basically our torture and brutality is so vast and so widespread that they want to legalize it.

13

The methods of profiteering

The classic way is for politicians to pass legislations favorable to the corporations who financed their campaigns. They may relax environmental laws, or issue tax breaks, or even a tax cut for everyone over a certain income. This method skews laws to favor select corporations and not the public.

Worse is the more direct method of profiteering. This is when politicians simply allocate tax revenue to be spent on companies that they have invested in, or that their wife or husband has invested in. Many companies are rewarded no-bid contracts, which bolster the value of their stock, and allow those in the know to engage in insider trading while maintaining control over the market value with the contracts. They can easily increase the price by signing another deal, and many times when the work is not even necessary or is highly over priced to do simple tasks. This is most often a method of the executive branch. The president's cabinet, with the possible exception of the vice president who is quasi elected, no-one is elected, they are appointed. Naturally, the cabinet is filled with CEOs or former CEOs, and business tycoons of major industries, in particular, agribusiness, pharmaceuticals, and energy.

Another crooked method of plutocracy, which can act as an attack on political opponents as well as serve corporate interest, is the age-old method of pork barreling. Congress will write up a legitimate bill and then attach completely irrelevant add-ons to it. For example there might be a bill about disaster relief in Mississippi and randomly attached to it is money for a project like building a new bridge in Iowa. If the bill is rejected then the media can claim that whoever opposed the bill was opposing disaster relief. And if the bill is passed then the congressman from Iowa got his pork project there by diverting part of the money that could have gone to the disaster relief or could have simply been saved. This is, by and large, a vice of the legislative branch, who like to gander pork projects for their districts. Adding to the layer of corruption, are the various lobbying groups, which should be re-named, organized bribery.

A solution for this kind of pork was the line item veto, which allows the president to veto only portions of a bill, and if not over ridden, pass the rest of it. The problem with the line item veto is that it is rarely used for what it was intended. Many times congress will go over a long exchange of compromises over a certain bill, based on legitimate arguments and concerns, only to have the president undermine the portion of the bill not of his party or not of his personal interests.

The most disgusting method of profiteering is warmongering profiteering

14

Eisenhower Warned us about the MIC

A vital element in keeping the peace is our military establishment. Our arms must be mighty, ready for instant action, so that no potential aggressor may be tempted to risk his own destruction.

Our military organization today bears little relation to that known by any of my predecessors in peacetime, or indeed by the fighting men of World War II or Korea.

Until the latest of our world conflicts, the United States had no armaments industry. American makers of plowshares could, with time and as required, make swords as well. But now we can no longer risk emergency improvisation of national defense; we have been compelled to create a permanent armaments industry of vast proportions. Added to this, three and a half million men and women are directly engaged in the defense establishment. We annually spend on military security more than the net income of all United States corporations.

This conjunction of an immense military establishment and a large arms industry is new in the American experience. The total influence—economic, political, even spiritual—is felt in every city, every Statehouse, every office of the Federal government. We recognize the imperative need for this development. Yet we must not fail to comprehend its grave implications. Our toil, resources and livelihood are all involved; so is the very structure of our society.

In the councils of government, we must guard against the acquisition of unwarranted influence, whether sought or unsought, by the military-industrial complex. The potential for the disastrous rise of misplaced power exists and will persist.

We must never let the weight of this combination endanger our liberties or democratic processes. We should take nothing for granted. Only an alert and knowledgeable citizenry can compel the proper meshing of the huge industrial and military machinery of defense with our peaceful methods and goals, so that security and liberty may prosper together.

Akin to, and largely responsible for the sweeping changes in our industrial-military posture, has been the technological revolution during recent decades.

In this revolution, research has become central; it also becomes more formalized, complex, and costly. A steadily increasing share is conducted for, by, or at the direction of, the Federal government.

Today, the solitary inventor, tinkering in his shop, has been over shadowed by task forces of scientists in laboratories and testing fields. In the same fashion, the free university, historically the fountainhead of free ideas and scientific discovery, has experienced a revolution in the conduct of research. Partly because of the huge costs involved, a government contract becomes virtually a substitute for intellectual curiosity. For every old blackboard there are now hundreds of new electronic computers.

The prospect of domination of the nation's scholars by Federal employment, project allocations, and the power of money is ever present and is gravely to be regarded.[1]

George Bush is part of a group of individuals who have taken this worship of money and power to the highest extreme. There are major flaws in the American experiment, which allow the greedy to profit from atrocities and covet power. One is the **MIC** another is the creation of **private central banks.**

First, there is the MIC, or what President Eisenhower called the Military industrial Complex. What does this mean? It is about the relationships between industries and the military.

Upon World War One, the world saw the rise of the MIC. This was the birth of the mechanized militaries. Planes and armored vehicles, complex artillery pieces, radio equipment, enormous naval ships, etc. are very expensive.

With the creation of the stock market, there is nothing to stop politicians from investing in war-related companies and then passing legislation that grants contracts to the industries they just invested in, or worse yet, are actually employees of. This is particularly true with members of the president's cabinet. Indeed, many cabinet members, basically, buy their positions by having their corporation(s) finance the political campaigns of the elected officials. They give big to both political parties.

The military is paid for by tax money or by money borrowed by the government from private central banks, (which is another hole in the system, I'll address in a minute). The military consumes over half of the discretionary tax money in the US. It has more money than everything else combined. There is no monetary incentive for the military projects to be cost efficient. In fact, it is just the oppo-

---

1.   http://www.eisenhower.archives.gov/farewell.htm

site; they tag on every useless bell and whistle possible. They involve as many companies as they can to ensure pork projects which often are located in the congressional districts of the congressmen who comply with the ordeal, mainly the people on the appropriations committee who allocate the money. There are missiles that are over a million dollars' a-piece, which have been used to blow up restaurants. There are jets that cost a billion each. The US spent 30 billion dollars in 2002 on building nuclear weapons alone. America already has thousands of nukes and it would be impossible to use them all (indeed the end of the world) and yet they build more.

One huge tax-free institution, which historically has always had a tight relation with the MIC is the Churches. There are always some Christian leaders like Pat Robertson or Jerry Falwell, who invest to the tune of billions into industries of the MIC. In return they spout propaganda to their flocks to support a war, occupation, or whatever the military is currently engaging in. These churches, for example, led the charge against the American Indians, the Communists, and today the Muslims/Arabs. It is not that it is an aspect of the Christian religion to wage senseless war (although an argument could be made), it's part of the Christian *businesses*, which are what these churches are. After all, you know none of that money goes to God, and less than a percent is spent on helping the poor. There is an intimate relationship between this faction and the Zionist MIC cash cow, called Israel.

Many people go on autopilot when it comes to religion or politics. So, here are a few empirical facts. Israel is a country that has government-sponsored terrorism, and the US supports it. They are a country with racially segregated settlements on land that is taken by force. Civilian Palestinians are shot and their homes are bulldozed. Israel is expanding its territory in the name of 'defense' through "Jew only" settlements, which the US helps to subsidize. Why does the US support this? Because Israel is a cash-cow for the American military industrial-complex which earmarks 'aid' to be recycled on the defense industry which US politicians profit from though equity firms such as the Carlyle group for whom former president Bush is a spokesperson...

The money changers, the people who have turned religion into a market, the kind of people Jesus chased out with stick/whip, (Luke 19: 45–46) have taken control over the billions in wealth that Christians blindly donate them out of trust.

15

The cash cow called Israel

More US foreign aid goes to Israel than to any other nation. In fact in 1997 more money went from the US to Israel than to the entire continent of Africa, in fact, seven times as much more! Even when nearly all fifty states, have climbing deficits and a looming federal deficit reaching 8 trillion dollars, the federal government sends 10–15 million dollars a day to Israel. Imagine if that money went to your state.

With the exception of Presbyterians, who recently divested 7 billion dollars from companies involved in the illegal occupation, other Christian churches are forking over billions to Israel. Ask yourself, whose interest is their top priority America's or Israel's?

The source of the conflict in Israel is on the surface religious but in reality, it is economic. The Zionists want more land and resources for their 'chosen people' the problem is there are people already living there. The third rate citizen Palestinians who are treated like animals have their property and lives taken away by the Israeli government. In an unfortunate backlash Palestinians are committing acts of violence against the Israeli military and the settlers much like the American Indians fought the frontier in the equally absurd expansion of Manifest Destiny into Indian land which was one of history's greatest holocaust. Tragically, innocent people are also killed by the suicide bombings, but it in no way justifies the systematic ethnic cleansings by the IDF.

The worst victims in this affair are the children of the 1074 Jews and the 3,734 Palestinians killed[1]—123 were Jewish and 704 were Palestinian.[2] On any given day you can read about some abuse Palestinians are facing from Israelis. Actually, in a time period from March 14, 2004 to August 31, 2004 there was a seven-month period with no suicide bombings. This was referred to as a calm peaceful period. On the last day of August some suicide bomber blew up a bus

---

1.   Figures based on September 29th 2,000
2.   http://www.ifamericansknew.com/

killing 16 people. It was all over the news. The mainstream media portrayed the suicide bombings as a return to violence after a relatively peaceful period. What went completely unmentioned on every single news channel was that 436 Palestinians had been killed[3] in the so called quiet six months. In fact in May of that year Israel destroyed over 400 Palestinian homes.[4]

Obviously that doesn't excuse a suicide bombing, but look at the context that was missing. Look at the total non-coverage of the Israeli military killing Palestinians many of them children, and demolishing their homes. Why is this unmentioned? Can you imagine how US citzens would react to an invading army that killed 436 Americans, wiped out our homes and shot our children? You can be certain Americans would strike back anyway they could.

How would you behave if your child were shot to make room for other people to occupy your territory? The idea of a Jewish state is as ridiculous as an Aryan state. I will have to agree with Einstein,

"I would much rather see reasonable agreement with the Arabs on the basis of living together in peace than the creation of a Jewish state."[5]

As someone that actually went to the PSM (Palestinian Solidarity Movement) held at Duke University Oct 15–17 of 2004

Rabbis of Neturei Karta travelled to Duke University to participate in the PSM Conference and demonstrate their solidarity.[6]

I can say it was a positive experience, an atmosphere comprised of Christians, Muslims, Jews, and Atheists. The focus of the event was divestment from the companies who abet crimes against humanity. Most of these crimes occur in Israel however companies like Caterpillar and GE have exploited labor and variety of other human rights violations stretching from South America to Southeast Asia. As Americans we cannot set the laws of other countries, be it labor or environmental laws, but we can determine whether or not we support them financially. This was the purpose of the 5th principle in the PSM that met so much criticism from lockstep opposition searching for a pretext.
7

---

3.   http://electronicintifada.net/cgi-bin/artman/exec/view.cgi/10/3054
4.   http://www.muhajabah.com/islamicblog/archives/the_clipboard/009164.php
5.   Ideas and Opinions, [Crown Publishers, New York, 1954], p. 190
6.   http://www.nkusa.org/activities/demonstrations/duke101704.cfm

Israel has every right to defend itself, however having a war criminal for a prime minister and continuing to build Jew only settlements, segregated high schools, and destroying Palestinian homes while building an apartheid wall is not discouraging terrorism nor is it an act of defense. Israel is certainly on the offense and is certainly encouraging terrorism. This is an American problem too; September 11th 1922 was the day the British took over Palestine. You cannot aim for peace while pointing a gun in your neighbor's face. Apartheid is wrong even when you have religious rhetoric loosely justifying your crimes with books (you wrote yourselves) that also advocate slavery and prejudices of all forms.

Hatred is an easy outcome of frustration but usually frustration comes from ignorance. Americans might be more interested in Mary Kate's eating disorders, Paris Hilton Sex tapes, Britney Spears's baby, or who Tom Cruise is dating, but it is our civic responsibility to educate ourselves about global affairs and American foreign policy. We are at war. We are at war not just because our inept president and a plutocratic political body of profiteers, we are at war because American people are willfully in the dark, too busy chasing shiny magazines and Hollywood gossip instead of doing some critical and ethical thinking. Capitalism can go too far—it is called imperialism.

These companies who profit from warfare, and who in turn, pay for our mass media with advertising, are milking the MIC. The MIC has the market power to manipulate manufactures. They can make companies by giving them monopolies, often over useless military projects—or break companies by awarding their competitors. So the MIC acts as an umbrella corporation. Everything down to the raw goods must in some degree, obey the military's demands. For example, a company that makes aluminum will have the military as their biggest contractor. Likewise, another company that makes soda or beer and needs aluminum cans is indirectly tied to the MIC as well, and so on. The MIC effects every major industry especially pharmaceuticals, energy, and science.

The relationship between the MIC and drug companies and then their relation to agribusiness and it's relation to the food supply in the world, labor, and the healthcare system, are topics mischievously hiding under blankets of silence.

---

7.   Photo by Lindsey White, Picture from PSM of Myself and Diana Buttu of the PLO

16

NAFTA, Drug companies, Agribusiness, and the MIC

Drug companies get paid huge by the military to create bio warfare and to make new plastics and materials beneficial to war. That is obvious, but what is less obvious is how drug companies are tied to agribusiness (factory farms) and healthcare.

Part of the reason why animals are on factory farms is because the harsh living conditions, which are encouraged by farm subsidies (i.e. the more extras you have the more money you get) cause a need for antibiotics. [Packing pigs in tiny pens right next to one another and in all this filth is making super strain diseases too and its ruining the estuaries.] These drugs (which would not be necessary if the animals were not so packed) are conveniently purchased, with money from farm subsidies, i.e. our tax money. These purchases are from selected drug companies which have business ties to the politicians that write the laws. In fact 70% of the antibiotics made in the US are fed to animals not people[1]. That is a lot of drugs. Not to mention drugs that are also bought as steroids to make animals bigger, and also as pesticides for crops and then later preservatives. Many of these drugs in the food are harmful which feed into the human health system. It is not just foods its other farm products with a less covert poison too. Just like tobacco, it gives people cancer and other health problems—then people pay big for drugs to take away the symptoms.

Mid West states, which are agribusiness centers, have a huge block of senators so neither party will bring this up. It is not just drug companies, a long list (cosmetics, heavy machinery, fast-food chains) of companies get paid through the farm subsidies via an artificial demand for their products created by the inhumane living conditions on the factory farms. It is as if the government was giving

---

1. http://www.boston.com/news/globe/editorial_opinion/editorials/articles/2005/08/08/antibiotic_abuse/

money directly to drug and chemical companies, which is communism. There is a reason it is called the FDA, the Food and Drug administration, they are part of the same team.

Factory farming and large agribusiness is not only used as a medium to funnel money to pharmaceutical companies, it is used to undermine labor markets and destroy foreign "Third World" economies. For example, look at NAFTA and relations to US agribusiness (free market my ass).

So, the Hype about NAFTA in the 80s was it would be a win/win situation for Mexico and the US. The US would get cheaper goods, thus allowing its consumers to save money and up their standards of living. In return, Mexico would get a flood of businesses to create jobs—yatta yatta yatta! Hooray!

Turns out that was all hype, actually careful planning, as this model has already been beta tested on American Indian reservations.

What NAFTA really did (and what we knew it would do) was to allow the giant US agribusiness to control more land which it could later lease to different partner companies, namely fast-food chains.

US agribusiness has nearly endless government backing so when they move into Mexico, Mexican farmers cannot compete with the American's government assisted monopoly. This drives the Mexican farmers out of business, off the farms, and into the cities, by the millions. That massive population shift drives down the wages in the cities because employees become so replaceable, and it destroys any labor movements. Mexico City is the largest in population density in the world.

Then the US corporate companies move into the newly populated cities and get super cheap labor, and in desperation many Mexicans try to flee to the US. And after farmers are driven out and the land monopolized by the US's agribusiness, the US can start leasing out parts of that farm land it doesn't need since it can easily import crops from the US farms. So they hand the land over to more US corporations, creating corporate towns by having the giants start driving out local markets. Thus the US controls the production and distribution of food. You all know how 'Walmart' works on destroying small businesses and business diversity/competition. You can watch it happen in American towns, especially in the South. Well, multiply that by 10 and you got Mexico under NAFTA.

In fact, present wages have dropped 30 percent from the levels they were at in Mexico Pre-NAFTA. The Mexican poverty rate has doubled. When you undermine the work force by flooding the cities from monopolizing the agriculture with our quasi-communist practices of farm subsidies, you drive down wages, which in turn drives down consumerism in general because people have less expendable income. This dries up the market allowing a concentration of wealth and a monopoly over products. The people who can no longer afford crafts and goods from small businesses, will be forced by their poverty, to get the cheapest lowest common denominator products from local Walmart-style stores, which have a complex way of manipulating its prices by auctioning its distribution services to manufactures who often use 'offshore slavery'[2] in China. (But that's another issue). Mostly small businesses are just shut down because they can't sell and certainly can't compete with US super corporations.

The wealthy simply don't sell the goods in Mexico; they manufacture their goods there with cheap labor, and then sell them in the US. But they keep the prices high, and why not? Just because they are saving on manufacturing doesn't mean they have to pass the savings on to US consumers. No, they just keep the increase in the profits for themselves.

And with Bush's tax cuts for the wealthy, they aren't even paying taxes. As businesses close in Mexico because the money supply is tight (from banks, yet another layer to this mess) and because the wages are low since workers are so replaceable, there are fewer jobs. This causes wages to drop even more as people are willing to work for less since it is hard to find pay at all. It just keeps cycling. Meanwhile Mexico has to pay off debts for the US' foods from their agribusinesses. Mexico can't pay it so what do they do? They lease away more of their land to US corporations.

The poverty has many effects, it leads to drug use and crime and feeds into another huge US business and that's the jail-and-court system, which feeds on the drug war. But that's too big of a tangent, most of it seems to be administered by the CIA, but if you write about that, as Gary Web did, you might end up 'Suicided' as he was earlier this year. It is an enigma to me how a man shoots himself in the head twice, (with one gun). It was obviously a murder.[3]

State orchestrated induced poverty and cheap labor causes racism. People unaware of the market manipulations in Mexico assume that Mexico is in poverty and has all these problems because Mexicans live there.

Riding on the wave of resentment and frustration is also racism. Mexican groups do not blame the American and Mexican governments for their ills, but instead they blame white people, they blame the 'Americans'. Groups like La Rasa (the race) and others just add to more anti-Mexican racism. Equally foolish non-Mexicans react to these groups and Mexican immigrants. They blame the

---

2.   stole that term from my twin brother

3.   http://www.prisonplanet.com/articles/december2004/141204webbmurdered.htm

Mexicans for their problems, rather than the Mexican and American governments.

On the US side of it, Americans continue to lose manufacturing jobs, while their own taxes subsidize the giant agribusinesses which allow them to out-compete all the agriculture in Mexico and elsewhere. This is the danger of creating super state sponsored monopolies. These type of economic land games have been official aristocratic plans since the time of land-lords and serfs. If you control the food you control the nation.

NAFTA is the real enemy. GW and his Neocons are the real source of the problem. Do not be fooled by fanciful titles like "Free Trade." Free trade is not really free or fair because it is not on the free market, it's the opposite. It's on the government sponsored markets.

17

Deception by way of Fear and clever Titles.

They love to give nice sounding titles to things which are normally the opposite of what they say. As Oliver Stone's wonderful movie JFK pointed out, "Black is white and white is black". When the US names something the PATRIOT ACT, it is the very opposite, it's a destruction of the Bill of Rights, the epitome of un-patriotism. When Senator Ted Kennedy recently tried to pass his 'Hate Crimes' bill, it had little and nothing to do with hate crimes and everything to do with limiting free speech. When the State of Virginia passed the "education referen-dum" which was colored in complex language to seem as if it gave colleges money, we come to find out that, no, the money is earmarked for construction. It just gave construction companies money to build fancy structures on school grounds. Oh yes, even schools are treated as businesses. But they pale in compar-ison to laundering money through agribusiness, pharmaceutical companies, and their related offshoots.

The government also creates hyped up fear campaigns to increase drug com-pany profits. From Lime disease, to the West Nile virus, to SARS, Anthrax, and currently the Bird Flu they greatly exaggerate or even fabricate a disease to get congress to hand over more money to create vaccines to non-threats. For exam-ple, Secretary Rumsfeld stands to make about 4 to 7 billion dollars off of these bogus unwarranted avian bird flu vaccinations and pills.

"Tamiflu was developed and patented in 1996 by a California biotech firm, Gilead Sciences Inc. Gilead is a NASDAQ-listed stock company which prefers to maintain a low profile in the current rush to Tamiflu. That might be because of who is tied to Gilead. In 1997, before he became Pentagon chief, Donald Rumsfeld was named chairman of the board of Gilead Sciences, where he remained until early 2001 when he became defense secretary. Rumsfeld had been on the board of Gilead since 1988, according to a 1997 company press release.

Rumsfeld holds a Gilead stake valued at between $5 million and $25 million, according to his federal financial disclosures. In the past six months, the global rush to buy Tamiflu has sent Gilead's stock from $35 to $47—amounting to a windfall of at least $1 million for Rumsfeld. And now, with Gilead collecting royalties averaging 10% from Roche's sales of Tamiflu, he is poised to reap more gains for a flu panic his administration has done everything it can to promote.

Gilead Sciences is no small-time biotech startup. Its board today includes Bechtel Corp director and former secretary of state George Shultz (Bechtel is right up there with Halliburton in contracting to rebuild Iraq)"[1]

---

1.   http://www.atimes.com/atimes/Front_Page/GK04Aa01.html **Rummy flu** middle of the page.

18

Rather than changing cultural ills, we drug ourselves into tolerating them.

Greater than all of this is the exploitation of the mental health industry, which abused more than you could ever imagine. This is something that might make Tom Cruise proud as he seems quite passionate about the issue. People say he acted like a jerk in a TV interview, well maybe he did, I obviously did not watch it, but I will say this, you can be a jerk and still be right.

Where we are over medicated for the sake of profit.

Ritalin the chemical lobotomy. Because the American Psychiatric association and the Institutes of National Health have decided childhood is a mental disease. http://rys2sense.com/images/ritalin.jpg

Drug companies are publicly traded companies, which mean their sole purpose is to increase profit margins. The only way they can do that is to sell more drugs. Stop and ask yourself something. Isn't it odd that prescription drugs are advertised on TV? Isn't a doctor supposed to say if you need drugs? So why are they advertising? A doctor is trained to prescribe a drug for you based on what you need and is supposed to tell you which one(s) if any to take. But, people are going to doctors saying that they want 'such and such'. If an honest doctor, who is not manipulated by kickbacks from pharmaceutical companies, does not comply, then the patient can ask for another doctor who will give them what they want.

Think about this, how many drug commercials do you see on TV? Even compared to 3 or 4 years ago? Depression, erections, dieting, ADD, ADHD, OCD, constipation, age, heartburn, hair loss, you name it, they sell it. The drugs are never made to cure you either. They are to be taken every day for all of your life.

Many of these 'diseases' when they even exist are fixable. But it's only profitable for drug companies if they can give you a daily medication. It is better for them to mask symptoms and not cure your illness, or worse yet to mask your symptoms yet create side effects that require even more drugs.

Drug companies are invading our schools. They are trying to turn teachers into psychotropic drug recruiters. 80 percent of the world's Ritalin is consumed in the US. There is no empirical test for ADD and apparently no other explanation for kids not liking school, not paying attention, or being hyper, so they go over vague symptoms and issue out the daily pills. There is a huge market for such drugs as well and plenty of room for abuse. All one has to do is take the legal drug crush it and sniff it and they can get the same effects as illegal drugs. So patients can learn about the symptoms, fake the disorder (since there is no empirical test) and get hold of the drug they want to sell.

How many spam e-mails do you get for different drugs? There are spam filters now but do you remember how bad it used to be? Count the drug and food commercials in a football game, Enzyte, Zoloft, etc. Normal everyday products (like food) actually are being made harmful to your health.

"Researchers at the National Institutes of Health have found a correlation between an ingredient found in shampoos and nervous system damage. The experiments were conducted with the brain cells of rats and they show that contact with this ingredient called methylisothiazoline, or MIT, causes neurological damage."[1]

No wonder the pro Bush crowd has shiny hair...It is not just everyday products, it is also our food. A lot of our foods in the US would not be allowed in other countries. Many of the preservatives in our food cause a long list of problems and act on us like retardants. We even have packets of sugar that say it may cause cancer on them. Our foods do a heavy number on us as individuals. In fact, we have enough MSG to mummify a person. Remember St. Johns wart? It was a bogus antidepressant, and a study came out confirming it was no more than a placebo. Well, they didn't show the whole study. What the study found was that when St. J. was compared to a placebo and an antidepressant. St. Johns wart and the other normal prescription antidepressant (Zoloft) had no more effects than a placebo on ridding depression based on the primary measures. In fact the Placebo did better than both in that regard.

---

1.   http://www.newstarget.com/003210.html

"They also found that approximately 24 percent of patients taking St. John's wart had full responses to treatment versus about 32 percent for placebo and 25 percent for sertraline [Zoloft]."[2]

Psychology puts the cart before the horse. Chemical states don't determine your mental processes, your mental processes determine your chemical states. You can juice up your adrenaline, libido, or make yourself cry (all physical reactions) with nothing more than your imagination. Unless you are a determinist that thinks your body is a machine set up from your birth like a clock at the mercy of physics (the physics we know about so far), then it would be silly to give so much weight to chemical imbalances, or not adding one's environment and attitude into effecting their chemical make up. I mean, obviously drugs will effect your brain. LSD is proof of that but so does your will. But, admitting that would require admitting (partial) personal responsibility, an American no-no.

At the threat of losing my readers to boredom, I'm not going to get into my (non-religious) philosophy about free will and consciousness. Philosophy and history were my concentrations in school. However it is too large a tangent to get into an argument about determinism, biology, and psychology. Media and politics are enough to write about. The fact that a placebo works at all shows how a person thinks effects the rest of their body and the inverse holds true too, exercise, breathing, even music, affect your mind in a noticeable way. The nature vs. nurture paradigm is another one of those detrimental dichotomies. It is not that drugs for mental health are *never* helpful, what I am saying is they are WAY over prescribed because of profit interests. People have even given Ritalin to babies!

These pills are the new expensive magic beans. You are not a machine; you are a living organism with constant interplay with its environment. You cannot make warm things feel cold, you cannot make ugly things beautiful, and you cannot make sad things happy with a pill.

Who hasn't been coerced into (or the attempt been made to) taking a daily prescription pill? Nearly a third of the males in American elementary schools are now being medicated for a non-physically testable disorder of ADD. I'm not saying the disorder is not real, it is real, but I would say a majority of the cases are bull. And I think it is just as curable with no medication. Mental health suffers the most. Psychological problems are not treatable with happy pills. For example, most research shows that Anorexia and OCD, are disorders dealing with control, not the fear of being fat or the fear of clutter. (Most victims are women with over

---

2.   http://nccam.nih.gov/news/2002/stjohnswort/pressrelease.htm

controlling environments or Type A task based pride folks who see renunciation as a form of winning against the self, who they often do not like).

The fact that most of these disorders are demonstrably more prevalent in women seems to lead credence to the idea that they are psychological problems rooted in our **culture** and not biology. Adding to this is the fact that anorexia and other disorders appear more in some cultures than others, and actually hardly even exist in some areas. Obsessive Compulsive disorder, Anorexia, Narcissism, and Depression make the top four leading psychological disorders. Might our 'appearance is king,' hyper consumerist culture be helping to create these problems?

There was an alarming 73% increase in antidepressant drug sales from 1998 to 2002 and a 167% increase in the use of psycho-stimulant drugs such as are prescribed for children loosely labeled with ADHD[3]. Psychotropic drugs pull in $12 billion a year in antidepressants alone.[4]

Drug companies gave Bush tens of millions of dollars. They gave almost the same amount to Kerry. They know how to stay on top. Just play on both sides of the fence. Remember that Anthrax scare that lasted about two weeks? The drug companies were given a fat old check and the entire thing went away. The anthrax, as far as all the evidence shows, did not come from Arab terrorists, it seems to point right back to our own military which might be another reason for its disappearance in the media, but as of now it is still speculation.

As I said before, think about all of the other over exaggerated, scare-the-hell-out-of-you diseases and threats like SARS, Monkey Pox, West Nile, or the Flu vaccine shortage, or now the Avian Bird Flu (or whatever the last one was). This is scare tactics to rush you to buying more drugs or for congress to allocate more money into the pharmaceutical company's pockets. Personally, I have never had the flu shot. I don't need it! In fact it can make you sick. These, 'yearly hypes' as I call them, were all over exaggerated money-makers.

What wacky new scare-diseases will they make up for 2006? Be watching the TV screen because they are coming. I, actually jokingly wrote on my web site, which was deleted by AOL back in 2004, that they would use the Avian bird flu as a disease in 2005. Every year just before the Christmas/capitalist season they will cook up a new one. It is always some new threat, from Y2K to asteroids hitting the earth, to exaggerated diseases. The lies never stop. They got to pop up

---

3.   http://www.ahrp.org/infomail/03/10/03.php second paragraph
4.   http://www.drugawareness.org/Archives/4thQtr_2003/record0043.html 8th paragraph

that 4th quarter earnings report on the stocks; it is the annual report of course. It is part of why Jesus was born five days before new years. (The pagan holiday was actually on the 1st). What with the public constantly being pumped up with fear, there is no wonder we have rapid mental illnesses and high stress.

Alcoholism would be in the ranking of the top four mental illnesses (and I think GW could be suffering from spells of being a 'relapser'), but it is somehow considered a *disease*, when in reality it is a drug addiction and should be treated as such. And yes some drug addictions are not chemical; they are psychological which can be worse. Many behaviors are reactions to our environment; one can't change the environment so they change their internal states. Sometimes it is self-medication against depression, never a fix just a retreat. The phrase alcohol and drugs is misleading because alcohol is a drug, a very powerful drug. By separating drugs and alcohol in our speech, we are suggesting that alcohol is a lesser drug. Just because it is legal over a certain age does not make it any less of a drug than other drugs.

Possibly the worse drug industry is the Tobacco industry. I was once of the opinion that smoking was its own punishment and that people dumb enough to do it deserved its effects. I made this illustration to further my point.[5]

Natural selection is obviously a play on the term in biology saying that dumb people are killing themselves so cigarettes are good.

The punishment doesn't fit the crime. It is not also just dumb people who smoke. Many very intelligent people smoke cigarettes. Why do smart people do stupid things? This was a serious philosophical question that I pondered for some time. Well, it's like religion, in that a person's level of academic intelligence has really nothing to do with it. People who smoke by and large know that it is unhealthy, that it can kill them, and how much it cost a year, its environmental effects etc. None of that matters. **Insecurity will win every time over intellect**. And the marketers know that.

If you ask someone why they smoke the number one answer is it's an addiction. The follow up question is, "Well, why did you start?" The number one answer is, "I don't know". But see they do know. They just do not want to admit it to themselves or anyone else that it was to be part of an in-group. Some go as far to say they 'only smoke in social situations' further admitting the peer pressure behind their choice. It is not like a person smokes one cigarette and is instantly chemically addicted. They have to choose to do it for sometime. How can someone know a product will kill them and yet do it anyway? Because instant

---

5.   http://rys2sense.com/images/cigaryt.jpg

gratification also wins over long-term understanding. And that goes for pollution, procrastination, over-eating and a large list of things we intellectually know are harmful but whose effects are not immediate.

The human being given the choice between escaping pain but causing much more later, or dealing with some pain but being rewarded later, will most often choose the first choice because foresight is processed intellectually, not emotionally. In order to truly understand the consequences of our actions in the future it takes an act of imagination. We have to imagine how bad it will be. But in doing so the imagination is painful so we avoid that too. Imagination is the key to empathy, sympathy, and personal foresight. Sadly, schools kill the imagination in favor of intellectual understanding only.

Tobacco is an addictive poison but it makes our states too much money so it is legal. Seriously, it kills people and we sell it anyway in local stores with your food and lottery tickets (a tax on people who cannot do math.) Profit wins over humanity every time. If it makes a controlled source of money then it will be allowed even if it is poisoning the population. In fact drug companies get to swipe away your life savings and probably much of your family's money too if they can kill you with cancer. It is a nice way for the corporations to end up with your wealth before you die.

Fear begets consumerism. Envy does the same. They want to pump you full of fear and envy because they are greedy. A healthy solution is to turn off the TV. *"Eating square meals and moderate exercise is the best way to prevent most ills."*

Why are we so depressed? Why do we use so many drugs? We have the most money in the world; maybe we can just afford the most drugs. No, it is something cultural.

19

The distraction of the shiny things... Technology's effects on self-actualization processes.

The obsession with image is tied to consuming time as much as it is property. Lewis Caroll portrayed it well in Alice and Wonderland, one of the best anti-consumerism movies/books yet.

The Time! Hurry! Run little rabbit run. You'll be late! What effects come from super busyness? The toleration of many forms of injustice, which exist in plain view, is not the result of a lack of knowledge so much as a lack of sincerely giving a damn. Apathy, greed, and no time, are stumbling blocks for compassion. In order to genuinely care or learn, one must have some time to reflect and afterward enough compassion/concern/empathy to motivate them to act. Ignoring problems, results from a need to distract ourselves. Problems that are not immediate don't exist. It has become "Out of sight...out of mind." Occupation of time can be a form of escapism. We should spend more time on personal betterment and fulfillment and less on quick comfort, pointing fingers, and acquiring money.

"As long as each one of us is seeking psychological security, the physiological security we need 'food, clothing and shelter' is destroyed. We are seeking psychological security, which does not exist; and we seek it, if we can, through power, through position, through titles, names; all of which is destroying physical security. This is an obvious fact, if you look at it."[1]—*Krishnamurti*

---

1.   http://www.katinkahesselink.net/kr/war.html bottom of paragraph 5

Religions and philosophies that reinforce the destruction of man's self-worth are feeding our psychological neediness. The average credit card debt in the US is ~$8,000.00 I have seen trailers with a Hummer parked in front. How did image (false image at that) become so powerful? How did the need to impress become deep enough to outweigh living essentials? It has already been mentioned how self-esteem is tied to consuming material but another aspect is the notion of consuming time, i.e. being busy = being important.

It is unfortunate, but for some strange reason, people have come to link being busy with being important. The more they have to do the better. If they don't have something to do every night they feel like a loser. If their job has them pressed they need to announce it to everyone like it is a trophy, I am so important, I have so much to do. "Progressive action? Oh, I don't have the time, I am too busy, it makes me feel more adult."

I believe people are seeking/have a need for fulfillment. Status, be it through shiny things or long titles is one poor method for this end. Another way is to run away from it, i.e. continuous busyness. I've asked people, "How are you doing?" and I get a list of all the things they have to do.

"We acquire a sense of worth either by realizing our talents, or by keeping busy, or by identifying ourselves with something apart from us—be it a cause, a leader, a group, possessions and the like."[2]

"That is how everyone in the world is. It is a combination of selfishness and apathy. Either that, or, a person is too busy...Humanitarian/environmental/animal rights issues are for bored housewives or people with too much time on their hands. (that wasn't meant seriously)"—Lacey Conner

Thoreau once said, "Some men fish their whole life, without ever realizing that it is not the fish they are really after." The process is more important than the product. The fulfillment in fishing or any activity is not in the ends themselves but in the proper balance of challenge and effort within the activity. Too much of people's lives are caught up in planning their lives and not in actually living them. As W.M. Lewis once wrote, "The tragedy of life is not that it ends so soon, but that we wait so long to begin it."

So many people place their life aim at an occupation. School, college, and nearly everything they do in their youth is set up for a job. They do not even

2.   Eric Hoffer, *The Passionate State of Mind* (1954)

know what they want to do, they just know that they need one. If they get a good one then they have success. And success means the ability to acquire the largest amount of shiny things or have the most onlookers.

You do, as they say, have to stop and smell the roses. Constant activity, especially if it is trivial, can distract one from vital reflection, and self-actualization. Live for the moment too, not just for the future. The process is more important than the ends of the activity.

To give a trite example, imagine you are playing a game of chess. Let us suppose you dominate a 5-year old. Winning is not going to matter. The value of the game is not in the goal (the ends) of winning, but in the process (the means) of the game-the challenge. Likewise, if you were to play a super computer and you lost every time, in a few moves, the game would not be fun. The pleasure in the game is derived from a proper balance of struggle and effort—this applies to mental and physical activities. (...Things like martial arts incorporate both) The goal is often just something to aim towards.

Ted Kaczynski referred to this as the 'Power process'[3] or a psychological disposition we have in ourselves, which governs how much value we attribute to our actions.

'Human beings have a need (probably based in biology) for something that we will call the "power process." This is closely related to the need for power (which is widely recognized) but is not quite the same thing. The power process has four elements. The three most clear-cut of these we call goal, effort and attainment of goal. (Everyone needs to have goals whose attainment requires effort, and needs to succeed in attaining at least some of his goals.)"[4]

"Among the abnormal conditions present in modern industrial society are excessive density of population, isolation of man from nature, excessive rapidity of social change and the break-down of natural small-scale communities such as the extended family, the village or the tribe."[5]*—Ted Kaczynski*

(Granted, Kaczynski developed his own much greater 'problems' but that does not give reason to just dismiss everything he ever wrote.) I think we can pick and

---

3.   http://www.unabombertrial.com/manifesto/process.html the entire page
4.   http://www.unabombertrial.com/manifesto/process.html paragraph 33
5.   *http://www.unabombertrial.com/manifesto/problems.html* (paragraph 47 Industrial Society And Its Future)

choose which aspects of industrialization are detrimental and which are not. One of the main vices from industrialization and rapid technology is the dependencies we have created as well as the natural processes with our environment which have been stripped away. Mankind's psychology evolved along side activities in nature which fulfill the proper proportion of struggle, and goal attainment, involving many aspects of self-actualization: intellect, creativity, physical, social, emotional, and most importantly autonomous activities.

Things will come full circle as they have before in the past. Mother earth will prevail in the end. Some of our technologies are burning the candle at both ends. They rely on limited resources or they cause irreversible damage to the environment. We need to step back and look at the full picture and impact with foresight and analysis. We need alternative clean energy and we need new outlets. Or we can continue to burn our air and water and have our armies fight each other over the dirt with the most silver/gold/iron/spices/opium/tea/indigo/oil or whatever the resource of the period is.

Many people have nowhere to actualize their potentials. Humans evolved doing X amount of Physical, Creative, and Mental work and most importantly Social—communal interaction. By breaking these ties, we are creating conditions for hyper competition and a backlash of superficial in-groups and creeds resulting as compensation. By making our values so lopsided, by neglecting some of our natural attributes, we are drying up vital psychological nutrients. In our culture, Arts, Music, and so on, are becoming 'extras' rather than 'equals.' Yet when we admire a civilization of the past, it is the arts, the sculptures, the literature, theater, architecture, poetry and so forth that we admire,—that is what sets it apart from others. We need to re-think our institutional structures that give rise to this slanted approach to life, which favors intellect. It is like we are on a chair with one leg too long.

Happiness is not so much what we can get, as it is our ability to appreciate what we have already got. Dissatisfactions are judgments in a relative stance to what we are 'used to.' We take so much for granted. What someone experiences as pleasing or displeasing is relative to their 'neutral point' A neutral point is where on the spectrum a person falls pertaining to the amount of things they take for granted, expect, or feel entitled to.

We take for granted simple pleasures like being able to have ice in the middle of the summer. These were once great luxuries before of the advent of refrigeration. Now, they have moved into the zone of expectancies. We require a certain level of things just to feel neutral and then we must add on top of that point to gather happiness. We start to require so much just to be neutral that we spend too much time 'running in circles;' we lose sight of more important things. Chiefly, because we substitute intangible acquisitions, in an attempt to fill our social void. Many adult social scenes center around alcohol, a drug to break inhibitions…So, how can we lower our neutral points?

Reflection is a good first step. With our imaginations we can remind ourselves how much we have to cherish. We can compare our circumstances with others in harsher times or places, or even hypotheticals. (thus a strong imagination is linked to a deeper ability to empathize)

But our imaginations can only take us so far. There is definitely something to be said for deep reflection and the practice of such things as Zen and Taoism, but these are very difficult for most people.

Sometimes, it is worth our wild to purposely hold 'renunciation' for some of our privileges. To live the warrior way, to garden, farm, or fish, [sleep without an electric blanket] even though we don't have to, at least, not for the products they bring. We value most what we willingly work for, and we value less what is given to us with out some sense of 'deserving' or effort that we had to invest.

People enjoy exercising their freedoms and their skills. We love to choose things and we feel the best with things, when we earned them. It may be a good practice then to allot a certain amount of time where you will reflect about things you take for granted and even deprive yourself of certain comforts for a time so that they will not be unappreciated. It is not to call the things you take for granted, bad or evil as some religions do. It is actually to do the opposite. Values increase as we miss things, as we lower our neutral points. Before we can have reflection we must make the time for it. We must also not be afraid of it. Too much time is gobbled up in the need for money—both for over-charged necessities and for consumerism, but in a different system it would not have to be this way. **Purposely remaining frivolously busy is a form of escapism** and it detracts from our time to reflect. This escapism is reinforced by the view that having "so much to do" equates with important-ness.

Reflection is about far more than, how we appreciate, and what goals we choose to pursue. Without some time to reflect on what we want (as opposed to what we are told to want/do) how can we choose which tasks to do? We end up repeating the same day over and over in our business cycle and wake up older in a mid-life crisis. We must break the association between busyness and importance.

Constant action is as bad as constant thinking/philosophizing. There must be a balance of thought and action. Also, the thoughts and actions must not simply be orders or cultural 'supposed to's', such as after college you get married then have kids, work, work, work, and then you die.

Bruce Lee once said, *"Balance your thoughts with action.—If you spend too much time thinking about a thing, you'll never get it done."* [6]

The inverse also holds true. Too much action leads to too little thought and ultimately, much meaningless action. We do not want to be armchair philosophers nor do we want to be mindless worker ants. However, the latter seems to be the far greater disease. Don't be *'just another brick in the wall.'* Find ways to make time—for yourself, (that does not mean escape in entertainment, it means finding what you really want, and knowing yourself) for your children, for others in need.

Self-validation is so vital. We must not look to impress others in order to impress ourselves. So many people juggle so many projects at once in our super fast paced produce and consume culture. People even eat on the go. What may I ask is everyone racing for? We are only in competition with one another, and there is no reason this hyper competition could not be switched with a system based on cooperation. People live like they are inside a hive. Like little bees, they work gathering pollen (money) for honey (shiny things).

Shiny things are nothing but shiny things…Human beings are far more important. Let us act as if we believe this.

"If parents love their children, they will not be nationalistic, they will not identify themselves with any country; for the worship of the State brings on war, which kills or maims their sons. If parents love their children, they will discover what is right relationship to property; for the possessive instinct has given property an enormous and false significance which is destroying the world. If parents love their children, they will not belong to any organized religion; for dogma and belief divide people into conflicting groups, creating antagonism between man and man. If parents love their children, they will do away with envy and strife, and will set about altering fundamentally the structure of present-day society."-Krishnamurti

Much of this results from our need to distract ourselves. When not at work, we lead plastic lives, full of instant gratification-at almost any cost, and endless

---

6.   p43 <u>Striking Thoughts</u> By Bruce Lee. Edited by John Little.
http://www.amazon.com/gp/product/0804834717/102–1287821–
1113736?v=glance&n=283155

hours of electric entertainment to consume our time. I believe much of this is caused by an imbalance of actualizing several neglected human attributes, in particular creativity and social activity.

Every human being has potentials to fill. Our potentials are of the mind, body, and creative spirit. To increase and exercise these brings peace and fulfillment, which is different than happiness. This is different from the kind of happiness that is just escaping pain. And the healthy kind of happiness is what I'm talking about. Most happiness as we know it, is escaping pain, be it mental stress or sometimes physical. Thinking about these things lets them sink in, (become processed) thus the need for busyness. (Ever hear somebody tell a person with a tragedy to "stay busy"?) But the busyness creates more of the stresses because it causes us to keep ourselves from reaching these potentials.

Most of the time we have no choice. We have to do school work and money work or we don't eat. Sometimes school work or job work can fulfill some of our potentials like intellect. (and I mean college not the rest of school which doesn't even do that) School is going to bother most the physical types and the creative types because as it is now school neglects these things terribly. We seek to be happy, in things, in other people, in all the wrong areas. Sex is also pushed and tied to self esteem, it becomes about more than just love, it becomes tied to validation, cultural validation. But that is too long a tangent. People have within themselves a vocational disposition. An artist must make art; a runner has to run etc. We need to meet our potentials to reach this fulfilling-happiness. A builder needs to build and a scientist must discover, a musician must create etc. The levels of imagination, curiosity, and creativity compel them to do so. These needs are what I call 'psychological Hunger'.

Each of us has a PH divided over many attributes. India, Japan, Native Europe and Native America, all developed action based religions and philosophies. If you were making tea then you mastered it. If you shot arrows then you mastered it. Archery today can be very fulfilling for the archer even though it has no strict pragmatic value. That is because the process is more important than the product. These activities are simply mediums for us to actualize our potentials.

With current society, many of the natural activities like hunting and farming and generally being outside,—which require a high level of skill in the Big 3 (physical, mental, social) skill, have been taken away—the human spirit still wants to act in these things. The products of these activities has been taken care of, by technology. We don't have to worry about hunger, thirst, or shelter any more. You can go to the store and get anything with little to no effort. I already explained how effort and goal relate to value. The big problem is the process has not been replaced and we are missing out on all that spiritual growth.

When people evolved we needed certain physical and psychological securities. Food, water, sleep, heat, those things needed for the body. We needed creativity to make tools and so forth so we could get those things, and then intellect to reflect on trial and error improve tactics etc. For the bulk of human life, we worked with other people and we exercised all of these attributes. Social interaction (not hinged on competition) is ingrained in our program. We love each other and we like the loving process. We had to divide our talents and work together. Today our basic needs are already there for us with minimal effort, and we know how effort links to value and thus pleasures. So we need new goals but more importantly new activities for us to work out these missing processes.

It seemed reasonable and a good thing to make our biological necessities an easy thing to obtain and it is a good thing. How was one to know the invisible effects of what stripping the process away does to us as people? It is fixable. But today we fly around without recognition of our deeper PH naggings. Our society compensates with vicarious living and a structure that favors only one of the Big 3, intellect. The imbalance leads to an unhealthy spirit, a person in need of external validation.

Loss of the social begets hyper competition. Loss of the physical begets power-seeking through groups. Loss of compassion begets the scapegoat under class for instant gratification. Loss of imagination thus foresight begets a rapid destruction of the environment for quick gains, loss of creativity begets social uniformity and fear of change and thus fear of improvement, loss of SA begets a slue of mental illness and so called chemical imbalances. You get my point.

The priority hierarchy is the biggest mystery to me. I know parents who will escape from the responsibility of raising their kids through work—kids that run from school for entertainment. People also ignore inhumane practices for the sake of consumerism and comfort.

I once had an argument with someone who wanted a diamond and called ME selfish for explaining the DeBeers' monopoly and their shady practices using slaves. I was just trying to say (if you must get one then) to buy from polar-bear the only non-DeBeers owned company for diamonds.

Why does humanity take a back seat to short term personal comfort? And chance for object-made status? If the system doesn't change we will continue to crank out depressed individuals. But, rather than changing the way we live, we change the people who dislike it by prescribing drugs. We know Americans are over medicated for the sake of pharmaceutical companies' profits.

20

Profiteering and Military $pending

It all comes back to the MIC. The same drug companies involved in NAFTA, agribusiness, and in mental health are also hired by the military to make biological weapons, sanitation chemicals and chemical weapons, the kind we used when we dropped MK77 on the city of Fallujah burning civilians and animals alive of all ages. Politicians didn't care they made money off of it. The media didn't care they were silent about it. The head of the military didn't care they are the ones who did it, and then tried to cover it up.

When politicians make money off of the war machines, the manufacturing of them and the sale of them to foreign governments, it is called profiteering. Over on anti-neocons.com we like to call it *'profiteerrorism'*. The US is the largest arms dealer in the world and also the largest military producer. We spend more on our military (51% of our discretionary spending or over half your taxes every year.) than the rest of the world spends put together. The US is an empire. We are the only country on earth with 800 military bases stationed in other people's countries around the world. Imagine Iran building a base in Florida, it would never happen yet we see it as our right to build wherever we see fit. Selling and investing in the production of weapons are only two of the main ways they profiteer.

Another scheme they pull is with earmarked aid. For example, the US will send conservatively about 10 million dollars a day to Israel. Israel is then required to funnel back 75% of that money on US weapons. They pay for their illegal and racist occupation of Palestine that way. This is yet another reason US foreign policies create hatred. It is also blatantly immoral. The US uses contracts as leverage. "Oh you want this aid package for food and medical supplies? Sure. Just sign this other agreement allowing us control of your resources." AKA oil for food.

But the greatest form of profiteering by far comes after a war. The government uses reconstruction as a medium, to shell out government issued no-bid contracts to companies the government's employees have business connections with or hold stock/assets in. Look at the current Iraq war and Dick Cheney's Halliburton (or his wife's connections to Lockeed Martain). Halliburton's stock price went from $33 a share to $77 a share in one year. They also obtained a no-bid contract in New Orleans after the hurricane. That disaster is another interesting 'mess' to say the least that I will have to save for later. I can't even get started on it. Condi Rice and Chevron/Unocal are another example. See www.opensecrets.org for a list of profiteers. It is sickening. Bush's cabinet is like a corporate wish list. I am surprised that site has not been "Patriot Acted" yet.

Note, it's not just the Republicans either. Though I must write, that these Neo-cons are, quite possibly, the worst bunch Americans have had to deal with in 140 years.

It is crucial for the American media to create support for the military. They never mention the profiteering or even the facts. The Iraq war is an excellent case study of how they operate first with lies then with killing and profiting and of course changing their story. There is more to the MIC, for some astounding numbers.

Think of all the positive things that could be done with even a fraction of the money the US spends on its military in just one weekend. The entire world could have clean water for what the US spends in three days.

Largest Military Expenditures, 2004[1]
(Military expenditure: in MER[1] dollar terms)

Rank	Country	Spending level[2] ($ billions)	Per capita ($)	World share (%)
1.	United States	$455.3	$1,533	47%
2.	United Kingdom	47.4	798	5
3.	France	46.2	764	5
4.	Japan	42.4	332	4
5.	China[3]	35.4	27	4
6.	Germany	33.9	411	3
7.	Italy	27.8	484	3
8.	Russia[3]	19.4	136	2
9.	Saudi Arabia	19.3	775	2
10.	Korea, South	$15.5	$323	2%
11.	India	15.1	14	2
12.	Israel	10.7	1,627	1
13.	Canada	10.6	336	1
14.	Turkey	10.1	140	1
15.	Australia	10.1	507	1
	Subtotal, top 15	$799.2		82%
	World	$975.0	153	100%

1. MER = market exchange rate.
2. Spending figures are in U.S. dollars, at constant (2003) prices and exchange rates.
3. Estimated figure.
Source: SIPRI Yearbook 2005, Stockholm International Peace Research Institute.

1.   http://www.infoplease.com/ipa/A0904504.html

21

History of the Federal Reserve, Who controls your money?

The second great hole in the system is "**Private central banks**." Most people don't know this, but the Federal Reserve is a private Bank. It's not Federal and it doesn't have reserves. To save time, I recommend watching this film instead of listening to me. Money Masters[1]

This is about a 3hr film, but it is a must see. Please set some time aside to watch it.

A quick history of paper money is warranted. A long time ago, gold and precious metals were used as currencies. Metal can be quite cumbersome to haul around so people would deposit their gold to the goldsmiths who would write them a receipt. At anytime the person could return with his receipt and collect his gold. Trade could sometimes take months of travel. Merchants began trading their receipts rather than going back and forth to retrieve their gold, the new owner of the receipt knew that they could redeem it with real gold by going to the goldsmiths. This was the birth of paper money. The goldsmiths figured out that there was no chance all the depositors would come back to collect their gold at the same time. They learned they could simply print out extra notes and loan them to people with out a threat. As the loan was paid off they would be making gold from paper. Because there was a risk to the lender, that the borrower could skip out or be robbed by pirates etc, the money lenders developed the concept of usury or interest. Thus the money lenders were making money out of thin air and then collecting interest on it. Lending out more than what was actually backed by gold is called fractional reserve banking. They calculated that they could print out three times as much money as they actually held, thereby making 300 units of gold into 900 and collecting interest on the portion they loaned out.

---

1.   http://www.themoneymasters.com/

The Catholic Church soon outlawed usury seeing as it was driving people into debt, and the money lenders could more than compensate for the revenue lost to thieves. This would cause a lot of problems down the road as it allowed non-Catholics advantages in the banking business and later a Protestant divide. That entire conflict was about money, keeping it in England, so as to be allowed to charge interest on it. It was not about King Henry VIII wanting to get a divorce, since his wives were not having sons and in all likelihood, he had syphilis, which you were probably taught in high school.

The money lenders soon discovered a wonderful trick. Loaning money to businesses and merchants was great, but it did have small risks. However loaning money to governments was even better. The collateral for the assured repayment were the countries' taxes. Rather than raise taxes, something that could stir up even the common man much like raising gas prices today, the government would buy bonds from the banks. Inflation is hidden behind loads of economic jibberish. Nothing is more profitable for a bank than financing a war, especially if its home country is not even involved.

In America, the creation of the Federal Reserve was a dark day in history. It was passed by congress by a three man voice vote in the dead of the night. Our largest bank and the transfer of power of who issues our money, controls our interest rates and money supply, was created. The banks can encourage borrowing by lowering interest rates. They can then tighten the money supply by reducing the number of loans and raising interest rates. Inevitably a portion of the public will not be able to pay off loans or have access to more loans to give them time to gain the capital to pay them all off. Those in the stock market may sell stocks or assets to pay off loans and when enough people do that the stock markets start falling and create a run, those not in the lead lose in the gamble. Everyone unable to pay loans in the tightening money supply lose their assets to the bank. And with Bush's new laws on bankruptcy it has become even worse.

Something not covered in the film is the way these Banks help create the perpetual debt systems in other nations, in order to control their resources and exorcize neocolonialism.

22

Neo-colonialism

∘ ∘

"Only after the last tree has been cut down;
Only after the last fish has been caught;
Only after the last river has been poisoned;
Only then will you realize that money cannot be eaten".

—Cree Indian Prophecy

A quick example of neocolonialism: The West controls the land in Africa via private ownership of the land, taken by force from long ago. That or it is bought cheaply from puppet governments set up by EHM[1] and or the CIA. They cause a food shortage on purpose by not growing it and planting some other resource like rubber or by growing it and exporting the food to Europe and then selling it back to Africa. They don't GIVE them aid; the "AID" is a nice word for Bank loans for Africans to pay to buy back their own damn food.

It is called a perpetual debt system. The medicine we hear about being given is to bolster profits for drug companies, the loans are paid back at the expense of destroying the African currencies, thus insuring cheap labor and a worthless money supply. If anyone one is saving, the savings will go down because of the inflation from the perpetual debt system.

The World Bank will give a loan for an African (South/Central American, Caribbean, South East Asian etc) nation to build schools and hospitals, BUT it will not give a loan to make manufacturing plants for African products. On the surface it looks like altruism. But if they build the schools they go into debt and they have no way to pay it with their short money supply. Printing more money would just cause greater inflation and destroy the worth of any reserves/savings.

---

1. Economic Hit Men (Jackals)

So, they lease more land to Western corporations for cheap to pay for the loans for their infrastructure.

IF they could have a source of money, AKA manufacture their own goods because they have plenty of resources, they could sell products all over the world and then they could build their own schools and hospitals roads etc with no loan or with a payable one, and they would not have to lease the land to Westerners. But when a leader starts to do that he has an accident. Another method of the debt system is for the neo-colonialists to create a different kind of crisis. Every government has its power rivals and the US will use the Jackals to incite a revolt or uprising in a country and then pay the mercenaries, usually with drug money as can be seen in the Iran Contra scandal and its connections to Central American coups. To top it off the US may then loan money to the other side to put down the revolt, or as in the case with Haiti, they will intervene directly and run up a huge tab for solving a problem they helped to foster to begin with.

This also occurs on Native American reservations in the US and Canada where the non-Indian power holds the mineral rights or leases the land from the owners cheaply after induced poverty created by the classic corporate town model, and claims the minerals. In the case of the Navajo/Dine who have the largest reservation, workers were getting radiation poison from mining uranium for a US company which never spoke of the ill effects of which it was fully aware.

"The Vanadium Corporation of America and Kerr-McGee were the principal owners of these mines and they have taken advantage of the Navajo workers. Not only with paying low wages, but by not informing the workers about the hazardous effects that uranium has on their lives."[2]

Here is an example of how the US treats even the largest reservations which fairs better than the smaller ones. Uranium was discovered on the Navajo reservation in the 30s. The US stole or killed the Navajo's sheep to **break** their **self sufficiency** and then force Indians into wage work so that they would have to buy food from and work for Whites. US companies control the means of production of vital necessities such as food and water. Super large agribusinesses drive out all competition with their deep pockets and highly subsidized monopolies. Then they set the cost of necessities just below the amount of payment of the lowest standard of living. A better life can even be found in the US military where many Indians end up.

After US companies force Indians into poverty by theft, violence, BS court rulings, polluting/destroying the natural resources, (like rivers and lakes) and

---

2.   http://www.inmotionmagazine.com/miners.html

moving in billion dollar industries with endless government backing (and tax privileges) which results in the control of all major industry,[3] they lease Indian land (from people too poor not to sell) and strip mine it using the coerced Indian labor. The coal companies have poisoned the water supply on the Navajo and Crow reservations. (Not to mention the radon released in the air.) But will these issues ever reach CNN or FOX? ha ha ha riiiight

Indians are not alone in this, most of South America and the Caribbean face the same propblems but they at least have some leverage. Rezervations are 3d world countries that the US owns. They are by and large work camps for the likes of Peabody coal and the US Forest Reserve.

As a personal pet peeve, to show culture insensitivity and an absolute ignorance of history, I have to point out a minor yet easily fixable problem: The Washington **Redskins**. This is the team for the Capital of the US (even though the stadium is in Maryland, not Virginia despite Maryland already having the Ravens…) I don't dislike the football team; I hate its name. The word Redskin is not just a slang derogatory term for Indians equivalent to the word nigger or kike. The word 'redskin' refers to a bounty put on the head of Indians. For one, Indians are not red any more than Asians are yellow. These are from White imaginations. Native Americans are many shades of brown to near white much like Latinos. I have never have I see a red person, other than maybe an Irish tourist who stayed in the sun to long on the beach. And never have I seen a yellow Asian, and I have been living in Japan since mid 2005. I suggest renaming the team the Potomac Warriors, or the 'is-corrupt' that way, an announcer could say, "Here comes, Washington Is-Corrupt."[4]

Honestly, it is as if the government gets a jolly little kick out of stepping on people. I remember watching the invasion of Iraq and right there in the 7th Calvary (Custer's infamous cavalry which was annihilated by Crazy Horse) was the Crazy Horse Brigade. It is true that Crazy Horse was a warrior among many other things, but there is no way this man would ever want the very same Calvary which butchered his people at Wounded Knee and killed many before they were stopped at the Battle of Little Big Horn, to be named after him. A better name I believe would be "lost to Crazy Horse."

---

3.   note: they are competing with populations of only 300 thousand people, the American Indians have no chance.
4.   All five of you Algonquian speakers reading this book will enjoy that clever play on words.

23

Post 'Election' thoughts, I blame the Public.

The morning after the second Diebold election I wrote:

"From Iraq to Enron Bush has lied about so many things and allowed so much profiteering[1] that there is hardly a place to begin. I'm no longer blaming the greedy pork leeches in our plutocratic political bodies. I am angry at the sheep that support them. It's the soccer moms and the Reich-wing Christian coalition with their 17th century morality[2] and simplistic black and white view of the world, who have been the lock-steps of Bush's army. A religion of scare tactics, blind faith, and fear mongering…a faith that trades safety from (a fictitious) evil, for absolute obedience and trust, begets a susceptibility to a political structure of the same vein. The Born Again cult is Bush's front line of wild-eyed 'save me-if I obey' fanatics. Revenge is what the funda**mental**ists[3] want and their anger is palpable and malleable.

Corporate scandals go unpunished and disinformation[4] about the war is ignored or rationalized. When it was clear even to the unthinking person that Iraq was not a threat to the US, that Iraq had no weapons of mass destruction or a capacity to build them and no links to 911 or Al-Qaeda, when the claim about Saddam acquiring uranium from Africa was shown to be based on a forgery[5], the general public ignored it. The rational switched to the age old rhetoric of 'spreading democracy.' The truth is most Americans did not care why or who we went to war with, they were desperately searching for show of force to repair their bruised egos. War has become an extension of vicarious masculinity.

---

1. http://news.bbc.co.uk/2/hi/business/3231345.stm
2. http://www.cnn.com/2003/US/08/15/nyt.kristof/
3. http://msnbc.msn.com/id/6396422/
4. http://hometown.aol.com/ten13society/RyonIraq.html
5. http://www.antiwar.com/justin/j100303.html

When Usama[6] Bin Laden knocked out America's two front teeth in New York City, many Americans felt for the victims and their families, however as can be seen by the egocentric reaction to the attack, many were feeling like there had been an attack on their pride. They felt small and vulnerable, the fear was so high and the sheep so convinced, that giant bomb proof cells were on the market and shaky hands were scrambling for duck-tape to survive the impending doom of the mythical weapons of mass destruction coming from an irrelevant country. (The anthrax scare[7] lasted about a week, pharmaceuticals got a fat check[8] and it all went away...) The egocentric spin was that Usama had 'attacked symbols of America', that he hated American freedom and it was the jealousy of this freedom that caused the attacks.[9]

What of our crimes? We simply ignore them. If three thousand civilians die in New York, it's terrorism; if one hundred thousand[10] civilians[11] die in Iraq, it's 'spreading democracy.' The most interesting thing is that Iraq had nothing to do with 911 or Usama/Osama

MSNBC reported during the election night results that the top issue for many voters was not the economy or the war on terror, which took second and third place. The top issue at 21% was 'moral value' issues AKA prejudice towards homosexuals. Two women getting married is a moral catastrophe while killing children in a war that was fought on false pretexts is not.

Americans suffered from a battered ego. Note the delight of the big & bad, 'Shock and Awe' campaign. "That's right we'll show'em." What of the 1,200*[12] and counting Americans who have died? What of the 8,000*[13] and counting Americans who have been wounded? What did the war in Iraq

---

6.   http://www.fbi.gov/mostwant/topten/fugitives/laden.htm

7.   http://www.tetrahedron.org/articles/anthrax/anthrax_espionage.html

8.   http://www.tetrahedron.org/articles/anthrax/anthrax_espionage.html

9.   Never mind American foreign policy, which assist Israeli terrorism despite worldwide condemnation, never mind that the twin towers and the pentagon were strategic targets, they were only financial and military centers of the USA. It's not like September 11th 1922, was the day the British took over Palestine. It's not like Usama mentioned the Palestinian conflict 35 times in his infamous letter to America. It's not like he recently made a tape referring to the US-Israeli invasion of Lebanon and the Israeli occupation of Palestine. Hey America's support of racially segregated settlements and an apartheid wall is perfectly fine because after all we are helping Israel 'defend' itself from suicide bombings which in no way could be the result of Israelis bulldozing down thousands of homes, stealing land, and murdering thousands of people, in their religiously justified ethnic cleansing. American's are willfully in the dark about this issue. CNN and company report every suicide bombing and only report Israeli aggression as 'killing militants' and terrorists.' Why because Israel is a cash cow for the military industrial complex.

10. http://www.guardian.co.uk/Iraq/Story/0,2763,1338749,00.html

11. http://www.washingtonpost.com/wp-dyn/articles/A7967-2004Oct28.html

accomplish? Sure, Halliburton-KBR and the rest of Bush's cabinet's corporate wish-list made out. Sure, the concentration of ownership over oil has increased thus raising the price of oil and the wealth of the monopoly chasers. Sure, the greatest threat to Israel (the only middle eastern country that does have WMD[14] and does kill their own people daily and has preemptively attacked all her neighbors, including an attack on an American ship the USS Liberty[15]) was defeated. But, how again, is this fighting the war on terror? Iraq has never attacked the US and no Iraqis have ever committed a terrorist attack in the US (unlike Saudi Arabia and Israel.)

There is no Jewish or Saudi conspiracy. The reasons for the war in Iraq are in plain sight. Corporate profiteering[16], control over vital resources[17], assisting Israel,[18] and the expansion of the military Industrial complex, all have a common thread: American Imperialism.[19] PNAC or the Project for a New American Century[20] outlined the plan from the mid 90s. September 11th was just the 'Reichstag fire' that the neoconservatives needed to divert the public anger and steer it towards their economic aims.

Both Kerry and Bush supported the Iraq War, the anti-civil liberty PATRIOT Act[21], the unconditional support of Israel, increased defense spending, and homophobia, although Kerry to a lesser degree on the last one which is minutia compared to war and ethnic cleansing unless you're a Midwest/Southern bible thumper. It is a sad, sad, sad, state of democracy when the president does not believe in evolution,[22] cannot complete full sentences consistently, and the challenger is a gold-digging, special interest sell out, warmonger himself. Of the two though, it was very clear that John Kerry was the sanest choice. At least he believes in science, he has a great twenty year record protecting the environment[23], and he was at least going to stop some of the corporate outsourcing and raise minimum wage some insignificant degree. George Bush is the worst President since Grant and possibly the worst of all time. The Democrats should have annihilated him. They fell victim to the

---

12. As of this writing 2,066 sadly I am sure it will be higher by the time of publishing. Figures from http://www.antiwar.com/casualties/
13. Of this writing 15,477 Americans have been reported wounded. Figures from http://www.antiwar.com/casualties/
14. http://new.palestinechronicle.com/story.php?sid=20030108083301551
15. http://www.lewrockwell.com/orig/margolis12.html
16. http://fairuse.1accesshost.com/news2/reconstruction.html
17. http://www.spa.gov.sa/newsview.php?extend.215260
18. http://www.kentucky.com/mld/heraldleader/news/nation/9222612.htm
19. http://www.alternet.org/story/16784
20. http://www.informationclearinghouse.info/article1665.htm
21. http://www.epic.org/privacy/terrorism/hr3162.html
22. http://slate.msn.com/id/1006378/
23. http://www.johnkerry.com/communities/enviros/compare.htm

polls of self fulfilling prophecies generated by the controlled media and chose John Kerry.

The media does not report news. The media is a business; it has become an entertainment industry. This is a different can of worms, that given the results of the Republican takeover of all branches of government, I don't have the energy to get into.

Americans need to wake up. Our plutocratic system of a choice between the millionaires style democracy has failed. Democracy is dead; it has given way to the manipulation of the lowest common denominator. Our schools are a joke, our politicians are corrupt, our media is complacent, they have become a circus of hacks and talking heads of angry little men and women. Tucker and his bow tie, O'Reilly and his 'factor'…they are like little characters with exaggerated personalities that search for punch-lines and shock value more than reporting the news. They want a reputation for entertainment not reliability and newsworthiness.

It's a very sad, sad, sad, state of democracy when people turn to comedy central and satirical cartoon shows to get more accurate information[24] on current affairs than from our papers and televised news channels. This is not an exaggeration this is a growing reality.

Why do we even have intelligence agencies if the president is not going to listen to them? The CIA knew we had no evidence of Weapons of Mass destruction, they told Bush point blank, not to include the uranium myth in his State of the Union Address, but he did it anyway. Bush just gets rid of dissenting voices. CIA agent Valerie Plame[25] was ousted when Joe Wilson spoke out against the war party's lies about nuclear weapons, Scott Ritter,[26] General Anthony Zinni,[27] General Eric Shinseki[28], and Lawrence Lindsey[29], Richard Clarke,[30] the list goes on, and any dissenting voice is silenced. How can we have a healthy democracy when voices of reason are punished, or any disagreement with the war party auto-labeled as unpatriotic?

We cannot let religious fanatics and Reich-wing propaganda and scare tactics rule OUR country. Our process has failed. It is time to take to the streets. I don't mean in violence; I mean in numbers. George Bush is Not my president. I do not accept his leadership of deception. I will not follow his plans for Iran, Syria and Lebanon. We are not a nation of idiots. We have the brightest, most intelligent and creative minds in the world. We still have some of our

---

24. http://press.comedycentral.com/press/pressreleases/
     release.jhtml?f=09_28_04_daily_show_bill_o_reilly.xml
25. http://www.antiwar.com/justin/j100303.html
26. http://www.informationclearinghouse.info/article7197.htm
27. http://www.cbsnews.com/stories/2004/05/21/60minutes/main618896.shtml
28. http://www.usatoday.com/news/washington/2003-06-02-white-usat_x.htm
29. http://www.pww.org/article/articleprint/2980/
30. http://news.bbc.co.uk/2/hi/americas/3559087.stm

rights[31] left from our Founding Fathers. It is time to exercise the first amendment.

All that is needed for evil to triumph is for good people to do nothing…Do not buy into to the "let's not be a nation divided," poison that the mass media is sure to soon espouse. We *should* be a nation divided, our president is an idiot. We need to take the power back to the thinking people of America and away from the greed and ego-feeding zombies of Bush's U$A."

Since the time of that writing (November 04) I have come to question whether or not September 11th may have been an inside job with help of elements from within a certain foreign government. It is a bitter pill to swallow but there is a mountain of evidence. Many questions must be asked, why did building number 7 fall down demolition style, when it was not hit by a plane? Why was NORAD told to stand down? Why was the government running drills of a simulated 9–11 style attack on the morning of 9–11 and likewise is it not completely strange that on the 7/7 bombings in London the British were also running a drill of the subway bombings?

This government has lied about everything. They lied about Iraq's weapons, they lied about torture, they lied about using WMD on Iraq, they lied about FEMA, they lied about the DSM, they lied about the events surrounding the Saddam capture as well as the statue toppling, and they lied about the Plame scandal. I mean we recently have had British soldiers caught dressed up as Iraqis with wigs and everything carrying around explosives and then killing Iraqi police in Basra. We have Americans killing and attempting to kill Italian journalists who would later break the story of the illegal and certainly immoral use of chemical weapons. They lie and lie and lie so why should we believe their conspiracy theory about 9–11? Was there foreknowledge? Was it planned? With these Neo-cons I would not even be surprised.

Don't reject this view point without first at least hearing the arguments. If you automatically scoff at this then please explain away all of the other known lies and give an account refuting the evidence It cannot just be based on a personal feeling that it 'sounds ridiculous,' because what sounds more ridiculous is the government's official conspiracy story of 19 hijackers some of whom later turned up alive. Here is just a quick fact sheet and some things to think about.

---

31. http://www.house.gov/Constitution/Amend.html

24

911/Associated Wars Fact Sheet

*Hamid Karzai, the new president of Afghanistan was a top advisor for Unocal.

*Hamid Karzai passed a bill hiring Unocal to build a trans-Caspian gas pipeline worth 2.5 billion dollars.[1]

*Unocal began a merger with ChevronTexaco on April 4th 2005 [2] and completed the merger on August 10th 2005 [3]

*Condoleezza Rice, now Secretary of State, was a member of the boards of directors for the Chevron Corporation.[4]

*Halliburton-KBR has also gotten lucrative no-bid contracts in Iraq for reconstruction.[5]

*The money for reconstruction, the cost of the war and two random aid packages to Israel and Turkey were all lumped on to one bill.[6] The MSM reported the amount of the bill to amount to 80 billion, but they did not report on how the money within the bill was allocated. The President wanted the Secretary of Defense to pick and choose how to allocate the money instead of congress, which is unconstitutional. Senator Byrd had a few words to say about it, and about upholding the constitution.

'The absolute bedrock of the people's continued freedom from tyranny and excesses of all types of authority is the power of the purse. James Madison summed up in a very few words the significance of this power in protecting the people's rights and liberties. In Federalist 58, he wrote:

---

1. http://www.ratical.org/ratville/CAH/oilwar1.html
2. http://www.chevron.com/news/press/2005/2005–04–04.asp
3. http://www.chevron.com/news/press/2005/2005–08–10_1.asp
4. http://www.opensecrets.org/bush/cabinet/cabinet.rice.asp
5. http://www.corpwatch.org/article.php?id=11560
6. http://www.cbsnews.com/stories/2003/04/09/politics/main548524.shtml

"This power over the purse, may in fact be regarded as the most complete and effectual weapon with which any Constitution can arm the immediate representatives of the people for obtaining a redress of every grievance, and for carrying into effect every just and salutary measure." …

"Just a few weeks ago, after months of stiff arming Congress's request for information regarding the cost of military action in Iraq, the President finally provided the details of the first installment payment totaling $74.7 billion. Of that amount, the President sought $62 billion for the department of defense. But the President wanted the Secretary of Defense to pick and choose how to spend more than $59.8 billion of that money. Congress was asked to provide this funding in an account labeled the "Defense Emergency Response Fund." Around Washington, this fund is nicknamed DERF, D-E-R-F. I can think of another explanation for DERF——the Dangerous Erosion of the Right to Fund. No, it was not flexibility that the President sought. It was control. It was power."[7]

*Vice president Dick Cheney was the CEO of Halliburton after he flunked out of college twice.[8]
*Dick Cheney is still on the pay roll and has millions in stocks for the company.
*Cheney claimed Iraq was involved in 911. He was wrong, however. Cheney told NORAD to stand down thus contributing to 911 himself.[9]
*Cheney had a mock drill ever so coincidentally mimicking a 911 style attack on the morning of 911, thus contributing to the disaster of 911.[10]
*The principle of a company in charge of security for Dulles airport and the WTC, was none other than Bush's brother, Marvin Bush.[11] He was in duty until September 10th 2001, one day before 911. What a coincidence![12]
*He was a director of Securacom a.k.a. Stratesec, a publicly traded company, from 1993 until the fiscal year of 2000. The Sterling, Virginia company provided electronic security for the World Trade Center and Dulles International Airport on September 11, 2001.[13]

---

7. http://byrd.senate.gov/speeches/2003_april/2003_april_list/2003_april_list_5.html
8. http://www.informationclearinghouse.info/video1018.htm
9. http://www.911truthmovement.org/video/hamilton_win.wmv
10. http://www.prisonplanet.com/articles/september2004/080904wargamescover.htm
11. http://en.wikipedia.org/wiki/Marvin_Bush
12. http://anderson.ath.cx:8000/911/hj05.html
13. http://www.whatreallyhappened.com/911security.html

Dulles is the airport where American Airlines flight 77 originated on the morning of September 11th, 2001. The company also had business dealings with MCI, now WorldCom. (who got caught for insider trading and still got contracts handed to them in Iraq even after being busted). The Securacom/Stratesec company was backed by an investment firm, the Kuwait-American Corp[14]

*Bertha Champagne, Marvin Bush's long time baby sitter for his kids was found dead in Virginia crushed by her own car. See—10/05/03 Washington Post page 3. Interestingly the death occurred on. 09/23/03

* Some of the most important and critical evidence in a massive price fixing scandal was destroyed when the WTC towers came crashing down. This lawsuit named the US Treasury Department, the Federal Reserve and many of Wall Street's biggest banks and investment houses in this scandal.[15]

*In 1962 Operation Northwoods called for the US to stage terror attacks in the US and blame it on the Cubans as a pretext for a war. [16]

*The towers fell at freefall speed suggesting that the 'pancake theory is impossible; bombs must have been in the towers which fell like a controlled demolition.

*Larry Silverstein, backed by a number of investors, signed a 99-year lease for the World Trade Center complex just seven weeks before the World Trade Center was destroyed in 2001. Silverstein already owned 7 World Trade Center which was also destroyed in the attack. Silverstein was awarded an insurance payment of more than three and a half billion dollars to settle his seven-week-old terrorist insurance policy.

*The same crook owned building number 7, which fell at 5pm in the afternoon from fire even though no plane hit it. Later, Larry screwed up on a PBS documentary[17] where he openly stated that they had it demolished. He said they were given the orders to "pull it"—the industry term to bring down a building by explosives. Apparently that one fell from bombs that somehow were all set up in a matter of hours even while the building was on fire!
18

Notice the bend in the middle of the top of the roof? That is done on purpose. When you blow up a building you bust the center first so that it falls inward.
*building 7 also fell at close to freefall speed.[19]

---

14.   http://www.populist.com/03.02.burns.html
15.   http://www.gata.org/howe_complaint.html
16.   http://www.prisonplanet.com/northwoods.pdf
17.   America Rebuilds http://www.pbs.org/americarebuilds/
18.   http://www.wtc7.net/docs/streamers.jpg
19.   http://www.911research.com/wtc/evidence/videos/docs/wtc_7_cbs.mpg

*P51 of PNAC written by Neocons in 1997 states: *"…the process of transformation, even if it brings revolutionary change, is likely to be a long one, absent some catastrophic and catalyzing event—like a new Pearl Harbor."*

*"*Between August 26 and September 11, 2001, a group of speculators, identified by the American Securities and Exchange Commission as Israeli citizens, sold "short" a list of 38 stocks that could reasonably be expected to fall in value as a result of the pending attacks. These speculators operated out of the Toronto, Canada and Frankfurt, Germany, stock exchanges and their profits were specifically stated to be "in the millions of dollars."*[20]

(Basically insider trading where some how they knew those stocks were going to take a dive)

* 5 Israelis were caught filming the towers fall and they were dancing in the street. In their van were box cutters, over 4 grand in cash and maps of NY. It just so happened They were all in the Israeli military, two of them were explosives experts, and their van also registered a hit with the bomb sniffing dogs.[21]

*Osama Bin Laden worked for the CIA as Tim Osman.

*The science behind the strike on the Pentagon by a 747 just doesn't add up. Steven Jones a physics professor from Brigham Young University, has spoken out about the collapse of the WTC buildings and how the official story is impossible.[22]

*Firemen on the scene report hearing explosions.[23]

*911 led to the justification of two wars with different countries which turned out to be lies. Bush has hired his cabinet and the DOD's own business connections to rebuild things they destroyed under pretexts fixed by the MIC, which they also profit from through private equity firms like Carlyle.

The smoking gun in the official 911 story is WTC building number 7. If you remember, three buildings collapsed in New York on September 11th WTC1 WTC2 and 7. Building number 7 fell later in the day at 5:30pm a few hours after the twin towers collapsed, and it was not hit by a plane. The forty-seven storey tall Building number 7 fell demolition style straight down just like the North and South towers, into its own foot print and was completely pulverized. None of the support columns remained standing and its steel core became a phantom.

---

20.   http://tbrnews.org/Archives/a048.htm

21.   http://www.whatreallyhappened.com/fiveisraelis.html

22.   http://www.physics.byu.edu/research/energy/htm7.html

23.   http://www.whatreallyhappened.com/911_firefighters.html

Interestingly the building fell at close to free fall speed. Brigham Young University physics professor, Steven E. Jones, clocked the fall of B7 at 6.6 seconds. Free fall speed of the building would have been 6.0 seconds. He has joined the list of academics, who have come out publicly to question the official story. The physics just does not add up.[24] Jet fuel is not hot enough to melt so much steel so fast if at all.

"Building 7[25] was the third skyscraper to collapse into rubble on September 11, 2001. According to the government, small fires[26] leveled this building, but fires have never before or since destroyed a steel skyscraper.

The team[27] who investigated the collapse were not allowed access to the crime scene. By the time they published their inconclusive report, the evidence had been destroyed.

Why did the government rapidly recycle the steel from the largest and most mysterious engineering failure in world history, and why has the media remained silent?[28]

Larry Silverstein, the owner of all three buildings in NYC that were brought down, admitted on a PBS documentary[29] that building 7 was brought down by demolition. Watch the video clip yourself.

Larry says *"I remember getting a call from the, er, fire department commander, telling me that they were not sure they were gonna be able to contain the fire, and I said, "We've had such terrible loss of life, maybe the smartest thing to do is pull it." And they made that decision to pull and we watched the building collapse."*[30]

The problem with his statement is that it takes a long time to set up explosives for a controlled demolition especially when the building has small fires. But the building fell in a matter of hours. No steel building had ever fallen from fire in the past and some have burned for days. In Madrid on 2–11–05 the Windsor Tower, a building of 305 feet, a 32 story skyscraper caught fire. It burned at temperatures of 800°C for more than 18 hours and did not collapse. The South Tower collapsed after burning for less than one hour.

Building seven is the wolf's tail peeking out from under the sheep's clothing. If it was rigged to blow, as the evidence points out, and as the owner of the building goofed up and admitted, then the entire government story stinks.

---

24. http://www.physics911.net/reynolds.htm
25. http://www.wtc7.net/background.html
26. http://www.wtc7.net/b7fires.html
27. http://www.wtc7.net/noprobe.html
28. http://www.wtc7.net/silence.html
29. PBS'America Rebuilds
30. http://www.pbs.org/americarebuilds/video_players/trailer_56.html

David Ray Griffin so aptly pointed out that the 911 commission report does not even mention building number 7! The way the government deals with it, is simply not to talk about it! The 911 commission is about as reliable as the Warren commission. Henry Kissinger who should be considered a war criminal, was the first Neo-con asked to head the 911 commission, but that was so laughable and his credibility already so bad that he declined, and the next Neo-con took the task. The science does not add up. There is an obvious cover up when the so called commission does not even bother to address the collapse of a 47 story building which fell straight down at free fall speed and was not hit by a plane. The government/media has flip-flopped its explanation for this a few times. The latest farce is that a giant deposit of diesel fuel was in the basement of the building and it blew up to take down the structure. Really, where is the explosion then? And why was the concrete in the building pulverized into powder and how was there melted steel?

The maximum temperature which jet fuel (which is very close to kerosene) burns even when mixed with oxygen is **1700**° F The temperature at which steel melts, is approximately **2500** degrees Fahrenheit. Clean up crews found melted steel in the basements![31]

Get <u>Painful Questions</u> [32] by Eric Hufschmid. Watch the video <u>Painful Deceptions</u> free, the author has allowed a web viewing for no charge[33]

Another eye opening book is <u>911: Descent into Tyranny</u> by Alex Jones

I do not *know* what happened on September 11th, but I am certain the government story is as full of lies as everything else they talk about. What I have no doubts about is the MSM is controlled and lies for the government. You can be certain that should the facts about 911 be shifty the media would never touch it. It is worth taking a second look at the stories, something is missing, something was too convenient about the event as it acted as a spring board into a war and it was something mentioned in PNAC as being necessary in order to get a war in Iraq-a key goal in Israel's "Clean Break" strategy.

The government seemed quite unconcerned with catching Bin Laden and obsessed with invading Iraq. Shortly after capturing Saddam, Bush even said he was not that concerned about Bin Laden. On March 13, 2002 he said

---

31. http://www.911busters.com/911_new_video_productions/MOV/ Painful_Deceptions.html
32. http://www.erichufschmid.net/ThePainfulDeceptionsVideo.html
33. http://www.911busters.com/911_new_video_productions/MOV/ Painful_Deceptions.html

"Ah, y'know, again, I don't know where he is. I, uh, heh heh, ah, I...I...I repeat what I said, I truly am not that concerned about him."[34]

Maybe the known CIA agent Tim Osman, who we know as Osama Bin Laden, who worked for Bush's father a former director of the CIA, had already served his boogie-man purpose?

---

34.   http://www.democraticunderground.com/top10/04/175.html number 4

25

Time for us to take some blame,
we are a culture of unconcern.

✦

We're all sinking in the honey gathered for
the queen.

"Cleverness is not going to solve the real problems of the world, like war, civil strife, poverty and the high incidence of violence. Neither is it going to solve the mental problems so rife in the modern world. Only wisdom and compassion can solve these problems."[1]

We don't need more money, or more brains, we need bigger hearts, we need to put humane people in positions of power rather than the fearful and the greedy. We know damn well how to solve many of these things. Will you live in compassion? Bruce Lee once said, what is needed is self actualization not self image actualization."[2]

Oh the shiny things, when will we be free of their power? "Plastic people and their plastic minds slick magazines and shiny faces, shiny cars, shiny rings…oh the shiny things they are the new kings and queens.

What is needed is not so much a change of government but a change of value systems. Solutions begin with the individual. It's not capitalism; it is capitalism in combination with a psychologically alienated public. People have so little self

---

1. http://www.taoism.net/theway/wisdom.htm under the heading **The Solution**
2. "Self actualization is the important thing. And my personal message to people is that I hope they will go towards self-actualization rather than self-image actualization. I hope that they will search within themselves for honest self-expression." P143 <u>Bruce Lee Words form a Master</u>.

actualization (making potentials actual with activity) that they often shop for entertainment; they shop for the art of it not because of the physical needs the products bring. They have so few mediums to exercise their intellect that memorizing sports statistics and finding the best buys becomes a game to run away from boredom. I'm not going to get into drugs and beer addiction to movies, people emulating movie characters etc and other forms of escapism. We are taught to fight against one another, against in-group after in-group. It's the old trick of divide and conquer. They want to create race Vs race, man Vs women, old, against young, South against North, West coast against East coast, sub-culture against sub-culture, Protestant against Catholic, Left Vs Right…It's all to control you.

When land and resources are owned by the few, the rest must by necessity find an income, they rent the hours of their lives just to survive. The time given in no way reflects the profits of their labors. Their human worth and indeed the worth of the nation is judged upon how much it can buy and sell. Production, not kindness, creativity, love, or any aspect of character determines the well being of the state. No, it is gauged by the 'economy', the stock market i.e. the conditions of the riches few. You are a tool. You are under control for as long as you worship material possessions. Be careful that what you own does not end up owning you. Out of a week with 8hr sleeping a night and 40hr working one is left with 72 hrs. Then remove the hours used in commuting to work, you are left with less than 72 hours per week of life. Who owns you? You don't. Many work more than 40hr a week too. It is time for a massive reflection about our cultural values. How could cash and flags become more esteemed than lives and the planet? My former roommate put it well on an anti-neocons.com blog:

> ""Values" is a word we hear used a lot in public discourse—and it's a word we need to hear. Not for all the usual reasons it's thrown around, but because what we value as citizens of the world is at the very heart of the question facing forward-thinking people: why is our society the way it is? We hear the litany almost daily—poverty, war, pollution, extinction, corruption, genocide—the despairing drumbeat counting off misfortunes innumerable. Why should these things be so commonplace in our world? The answer relates to the cultural values we hold dear, noticed or unnoticed, and that we allow to inspire all our works and institutions. To understand why our society is one committed to social inequality and ecological degradation we need to understand the values that shape our society.
>
> The individuals most acclaimed in our society are generally the wealthiest among us. To become wealthy is considered a goal all by itself—not as a means to an end and certainly not as a means to help others. People don't acquire money for the purpose of using it to better society; they acquire it to make their own lives bet-

ter. The morality of this is barely questioned, if at all. When somebody buys a yacht we don't hear people clucking their tongues and muttering "shameful" they way they do if they see a couple sharing a passionate kiss in public. Where are people's priorities when public affection is derided as immoral but selfish extravagance is considered a harmless indulgence or worse, an ambition to be lauded? Intense debate on moral values is aroused by nudity on television but hardly a thought is given to the values that encourage people to enrich themselves at the expense of others.

The exposure of the human body on TV isn't disgusting, it's disgusting to see the modern executive aristocracy enjoying standards of living beyond the greediest dreams of emperors and kings while the average employees of their billion-dollar businesses snatch like fish in a tank for the scraps "trickled down" to them. And we're given nothing better to want than to be just like those plutocrats (just as they had nothing better to want than to become what they are). Thousands plunge themselves into credit debt in an attempt to achieve the lifestyles modeled by the rich. In an entire system based on greed, the cost goes beyond what's written on price tags. A society that awards esteem to those who accumulate the community's wealth in their own hands encourages them to do so at the cost of societal well-being. Because people have every reason they can conceive of within the framework of our cultural delusion to go on accumulating wealth they will do so and manipulate the system to allow them to do so as much as possible.

A typical five year-old will squeal with delight when given a few dollars but when presented with a spider or beetle, the child will often squash it without hesitation. This illustrates the absorption of a twisted set of values. The values that encourage our assault on the natural world and each other are relentless in our culture."[3]

It is important to see how the value systems are reinforced by religious doctrines, at least in regards for the major old world religions. I would note that Native American philosophies and things such as Taoism and a variety of pantheist faiths are the few exceptions.

"We are taught that the planet is inert, plants are insensate, and animals are incognizant. We are taught that our own bodies are crude and inappropriate. This fallacious bifurcation of the mind from the world it inhabits encourages all manner of destruction. The essential assumption of our society is that sapience, that most characteristic trait of humankind, earns our species the right to strive for complete mastery over the physical world. This idea, that it is the special purview of humanity to own the land, control its resources, and command the very forces of nature, drives us to extremely self-endangering behavior. Vital ecological systems

---

3.   A Perspective on Values and Social Change by Mike Murphy http://www.rys2sense.com/anti-neocons/viewtopic.php?p=6611#6611

are dismantled in the name of human growth and it isn't perceived as problematic because the human mind is something other than the rest of the world; something higher. The casual threads that connect us to the rest of the whole aren't truly acknowledged and we can therefore act upon the plant without seeing how we ourselves are affected. The perceptual disjunction of humankind from the world is embodied in so many of our philosophies and institutions it is all but invisible by virtue of its ubiquity. Politicians and economists refer to complex communities of interrelating life as "resources" and nearly all of the major religions write the Earth off as a prologue to an infinite afterlife or call it a painful illusion to be transcended. We reduce the global community of life that molded our species to abstractions and in denying its subjective existence make it that much easier to behave as if the whole of creation was set into motion for our sole benefit. Among the results is an anthropogenic mass extinction on a scale equal to that of an asteroid impact with all that that implies for the future welfare of humanity. Clearly what we value is not life—neither our own children's nor that of the rest of the biosphere"

It is beyond apparent that change is needed in what we as a society value. Part of the problem with this is that change has become equated with sacrifice. People don't want to sacrifice what they have come to believe is good about their lives. Change needs to be recast as something that gains everyone something. If people understood what they lack in their lives, change would be seen as a positive thing. People need to understand they are actually being deprived. They are being deprived of a truly satisfying way of life and offered such a poor substitute that they are driven half mad. Living in our surreal culture where so many problems are taken for granted, is it any wonder that the majority of the American electorate has given up on our politicians as demonstrated by their apathy in the face of the ballot? Is it any wonder that we see people screaming in line in fast food restaurants just because their order was messed up? Is it any wonder our children have nothing better to want than to sit hour after hour in front of video games enacting violent fantasies of domination to combat the powerlessness that has become so deeply a part of their lives they can't even conceptualize an alternative? Is this what we deserve?"[4]

What must be realized is that insecurity not stupidity is the real culprit behind our plastic value system. It is not that people simply do not know about blatant fixable injustices and destructive practices; it is that they do not care. The ignorance is willful; people do not care to know. Invalidation is so strong, that each tool prefers the pecking order society in order to remain above the unfortunate ones below them and also to have the pipe dream of emulating the princes and princesses. There are plenty of intelligent people who do nothing and care noth-

---

4.   A Perspective on Values and Social Change by Mike Murphy http://www.rys2sense.com/anti-neocons/viewtopic.php?p=6611#6611 3d and 4th paragraphs

ing for political affairs. Retreating to private comforts suits them fine so long as they are not immediately effected and so long as the effects that do come are never related, due to willful ignorance, back to their origins of greater injustices.

So many possessions have value because of their perceived value from others. It was Oscar Wilde who once said, "*Fashion is a form of ugliness so intolerable that we have to alter it every six months.*" But if we are going to fix this it will not be with education. People of all levels of education chase after shiny things and cooked up fashions. As I stated before, the problem is neither stupidity nor ignorance, it is insecurity and at the root of insecurities are religions of invalidation. Even an atheist is subject to a surrounding culture polluted by religious invalidation and division of man and planet.

We have new gods as well-they are called celebrities. The beautiful people have a dual function. They serve as entertainment but also (for most) an impossible standard of comparison which covertly dismantle self image but creates a compensation of the disparities via fashion and product emulation. Insecurity is the mother of excess, and it is the absurd level of excess which has created the horrible neglect for the health of the planet and other humans. The numbers are astounding. **Insecurity** begets a pursuit for **excess** in order to validate one's self through possessions. Excess leads to our reoccurring historical theme of injustices (preventable poverty, exploitations, warfare, corporatism, pollution etc.) the harmful domination over nature and mankind.

> "* As the gap between rich and poor grows wider, the 225 richest people in the world now own assets worth more than $1 trillion (that's a million million dollars!). That equals the annual income of 47% of the entire world's population (or 2.5 billion people!).
>
> * In the United States since 1977, the richest 1% of American households have doubled their share of our nation's wealth. The United States now has, by far, the most unequal distribution of wealth of any major country on earth.
>
> * The richest 1% of the population now owns as much wealth as the bottom 95% of all Americans combined. The richest 5% of American households own more than 60% of our nation's household wealth."[5]

---

5. http://bernie.house.gov/economy/today.asp in the ***Who's Winning*** section.

26

The good news! The Neocons ship is sinking and sinking fast

It is sick. Bush is part of a group which has many names; I just call it the NWO or New World Order. They actually aim at globalization and world domination. Watching these characters fall apart even without any MSM coverage has been a joyous pleasure. The first major crack in the Neo-con's warship came from the Fitzgerald torpedo. Patrick Fitzgerald is the lawyer who indicted Libby and is handling the "Plame Affair" or the case of the ousted CIA agent.

Now for the fun part, (some good news) reveling in the inevitable sinking Neo-con ship. It has been fun to watch this monstrously underrated case unfold from the lonely seat in the alternative media theatre. It is time for the peace party to break out the popcorn and butter because the Neo-con cabal is already limping on its wounded Achilles heel.

With all their money and power and control over the press, one would wonder how we would ever bring them down. Well, as history shows, empires fall victim to their own hubris. The sloppy Niger forgeries are blanketed in assurance and arrogance. They did not bother with doing the ten minutes of research it would take to figure out they had the wrong signature on the document they were faking. They had no worries because big government had already set its course of action to go to war with Iraq, the forgers were simply giving ad hoc justifications to an administration they already knew agreed with them. They were not attempting to fool the US government; they knew everyone was in on it together and did not think they had to worry about being uncovered.

It sure is biting them in the ass now. Let us delve deeper into the story of the Plame Affair. This case is far more important than blowing the cover of an undercover CIA agent. You have to ask, why was her cover blown? The answer is simple. But first some background.

Lord Bush and his merry band of Zionists created a group called the OSP the Office of Special Plans. The OSP was embedded in the DOD (department of defense). The purpose of the OSP was to make a case for a war against Iraq. They were to use scare tactics and lies to achieve these ends.

Because it is a logical fallacy to try and disprove a negative, the WMD claim was a great myth. It could be later said after the war, that it was a "mistake" rather than a lie. There was also no way for Iraq to prove they **didn't** have something. That is why the burden of proof is supposed to be on the party making the assertion of a positive not a negative. I don't have to prove that unicorns don't exist in Virginia, you would have to prove that they do. The default setting is that they don't, until proven otherwise. But, with Iraq, the default setting was they had WMDs, even though no one had ever seen them and there was no physical evidence for them.

Iran is stuck in the same witch trial as Iraq. The war party has two illogical flaws in their arguments. Iran is guilty until proven innocent and just like Iraq, Iran is being told to prove a negative. They have to prove they are not doing something. Iraq had to prove they did not have weapons of mass destruction. It turns out that they did not have any but how can you show some one you do not have something. The accuser can endlessly claim you are hiding them. There is nothing you can produce to show you do not have something. All one can do is allow the inspectors in which both Iraq and Iran did. The tricky propaganda with Iraq was that the American inspectors had to be removed. American talk radio and the MSM claimed they were kicked out. The truth is that our inspectors were caught doubling as spies for the CIA. The US removed its own inspectors. The conditions of surrender for Iraq in the first gulf war were that economic sanctions, which starved and killed thousands of innocent children, would not be removed until Iraq disarmed. Well, Iraq did disarm and the US drew back the deal and upped the ante. The US wanted a regime change, someone who was more US and Israeli friendly. This was never explained. The picture was painted that Iraq threw out the weapons inspectors, thus creating the suspicion that they must have been hiding something.

All international inspectors came up with nothing and the US never had any physical evidence that Iraq was building or possessed any WMD. Just to add emotional smoke to the mix the US media and government piled lies on top of lies about Saddam and Al Qaeda connections and links to Iraq and September eleventh. None of these things were true but they kept the public in line long enough to get the war going and it stifled debate. The rhetoric finally settled on spreading democracy (at gun point) in order to, in Bush's theory; create states that had conditions more resistant to breeding terrorists. (Ironically we have done the opposite; we created theocracies rigidly divided along religious and ethnic lines and an endless breeding ground for terrorists.) Well, as flawed as that is, it would not matter even if it was true because the LEGAL reason for the war were UN resolution 1441 which stated that Iraq could not have WMD, and they did not have any, so the war was illegal. Spreading democracy by force is no more valid a reason to start a war than is spreading communism or manifest destiny.

At best, the war party could claim that they made huge mistakes and miscalculations. However, this defense fell apart after the war party was caught faking documents about Iraq's ambitions for uranium. The war party media fed us a steady dose of manufactured fear. The coined phrase was we could not gamble with the WMD, because we could not let the smoking gun be a mushroom cloud. These claims were outrageous. It is interesting that even though the claims about Iraq acquiring yellowcake uranium were false and easily proven faked, there was already this huge media package and propaganda from the talking heads about the threat of the nuclear bomb. They kept repeating their catch phrases Goebbelian style.

Many of the lies the OSP told were about things that could not be disproved only proven. Over enough time ad-hoc hypotheses get old, eventually even the president had to admit that Iraq was never producing nor did they possess weapons of mass destruction. No material evidence ever supported the claims about Saddam and 911 or Al Qaeda either. But at one time the OSP actually tried to make physical evidence, something that finally was more than just hear-say. This is what will do them in because the prior rhetoric can be shamelessly blamed on mistaken information, even when the war party professed to be certain of it. Cheney went as far to say as there was no doubt about it. George Tenet had to later come out and say they were all wrong and then resign. Well as transparent as those lies are, one of the Neocons' fabrications can not be excused by saying "oh whups." This is because we have a documented crude forgery.

The death nail for the Neocons was their own hubris. The bogus claim was that Saddam was trying to buy yellowcake uranium from Niger to make a nuclear bomb. The proof they wanted to offer was from a document[1] that they forged between Iraq and Niger for the yellowcake. Here is where the OSP messed up huge. The document that they forged[2] a signature on was not only a fake; it had the wrong official's name on it![3]

1.   http://www.rys2sense.com/anti-neocons/viewtopic.php?t=453
2.   http://www.sundayherald.com/print35264

"* *In a letter from the President of Niger a reference is made to the constitution of May 12, 1965—but the constitution is dated August 9, 1999;*

** Another letter purports to be signed by Niger's foreign minister, but bears the signature of **Allele Elhadj Habibou**, the minister between 1988–89;*

* An obsolete letterhead is used, including the wrong symbol for the presidency, and references to state bodies such as the Supreme Military Council and the Council for National Reconciliation are incompatible with the letter's date;

* It wasn't until just before the war began that Mohamed El Baradei, IAEA director-general, told the UN Security Council on March 7 that his team and 'outside experts', had worked out that 'these documents…are in fact not authentic'."[4] (Emphasis added)

But was this in the main stream news? I never saw it did you? Thank goodness for the internet.[5]

The CIA asked Bush not to include this in his State of the Union address. Because this was proof that 'intelligence' was being fixed. You can combine that with the DSM which said back in July 23 of 2002 to rig propaganda which would allow public support for a war with Iraq. The OSP was the faction in charge of the lying. They worked with the INC (Iraqi National Congress) mainly through captain bullshit himself Ahmed Chalabi. As I wrote in Oct 20th 2005 [6]

The OSP WHIGs used the Iraqi National congress's bogus fabrications ringlead by Chalabi, as a pretext and a scare tactic to get the US public and international bodies to support a war. The US media was COMPLETELY in bed with the administration on this. They were like little cheerleaders repeating the lies which came from one source leading up to their jack-off-missile-Jonny 'Shock and Awe' bombing campaign. Wolf Blitzer from CNN, a former AIPAC employee, couldn't hide it. He couldn't keep himself from smiling. He must have said "Shock and Awe" with delight over 50 times.

Lewis Libby was[7] Dick Cheney's chief of staff an OSP member and PNAC co-author. Replace "supporter" with "co-author" It turns out that in the scandal

---

3. http://cryptome.org/niger-docs.htm
4. http://www.globalresearch.ca/index.
    php?context=viewArticle&code=MCK20030713&articleId=498 starting on the 8th paragraph
5. http://www.rys2sense.com/anti-neocons/viewtopic.php?t=453
6. http://www.rys2sense.com/anti-neocons/viewtopic.php?t=645
7. Patrick Fitzgerlad's indictment has since forced him to resign.

with Karl Rove and Valerie Plame that Judith Miller's source for the CIA agent identity was Lewis Libby. She went to jail rather than give up her source of a man who purposely leaked info about the CIA agent to blow her cover. Miller, if you remember, was the journalist for the New York Time who wrote the whopper about Saddam buying Aluminum tubes to be used as centrifuges, which was not only untrue but would not even physically work even if it was true.

The question becomes **WHY?** Well Plame's husband Joe Wilson was being critical about the evOIL empire's claims on Weapons of Mass Destruction especially concerning the uranium myth. The main stream media tried to spin the entire case into being about personal revenge against Joe Wilson. But it was about far more than simply bitter revenge. Plame (as a clandestine agent) was in a position to uncover who forged the Niger Documents. They had to get rid of her.

Lord Bush included the 'Saddam is building a nuke' lies in his State of the union address. Which have now become his infamous 16 words.

"The British government has learned that Saddam Hussein recently sought significant quantities of uranium from Africa"—State of the Union Address 2003[8]

For the record, the British got their information from the Italians who appear to have gotten it from culprits working for Israel. In my speculation the missing character is Michael Ledeen, who was a top advisor to Rove and a couple of X CIA lackeys who manufactured the crude forgeries and passed them on up Cheney's OSP stove pipe to the President.

Larry Johnson[9] and Justin Raimondo[10] have also pointed the finger at Ledeen. www.antiwar.com's author and the editorial director Justin Raimondo[11] wrote[12] about the larger implication of the Plame affair TWO YEARS AGO! Give this man his credit and listen to him in the future. The Site www.whatreallyhappened.com has been talking about the OSP and the Israeli spy-ring until they are blue in the face for years.[13] Many of us have been shouting about this stuff for a long time now. Fitzgerald is only warming up, the trials ahead

---

8.   http://www.whitehouse.gov/news/releases/2003/01/20030128–19.html (*20 paragraphs from the bottom*)
9.   http://www.tpmcafe.com/story/2005/10/10/20458/059
10.   The editorial director of www.antiwar.com
11.   http://en.wikipedia.org/wiki/Justin_Raimondo
12.   http://www.antiwar.com/justin/j100303.html
13.   http://www.whatreallyhappened.com/archives/cat_coverupdeceptions.html

could ruin AIPAC and make the Big heads roll; we are talking about impeachment and jail time.

[14] ***Go get them Fitzgerald!***

Break out the chips and dip the Neocons/Zionist are falling apart and the involvement of Israel behind the US's propaganda for the Iraq War is becoming exposed. We KNOW Israel was spying on the US via Larry Franklin. Soon because of pressure alternative media and great anti-neocons everyone will learn about the OSP and its Zionist ties to the Israeli Clean Break dream for greater Israel and Klan PNAC.

Let's enjoy watching them drop one by one. Rove, a quiet bigger fish, is forever scared and falling. Libby will soon flop down and bring with him, most likely Ledeen and eventually on up Cheney and the rest of the Cabal.[15]

The crucial question does still remain, 'Who forged the Niger documents?' It is not yet a fact, but I highly suspect Michael Ledeen. A former military intelligence and CIA counterterrorism officer Philip Giraldi concurs. Scott Horton reported:

"As transcribed by Justin Raimondo earlier[16] in the week, Giraldi confirmed to me that former[17] (?) fascist secret warrior[18] and neoconservative writer Michael Ledeen and his CIA buddies were the origin of the forged Niger uranium documents[19] used[20] by the administration to fool[21] Americans into supporting the invasion of Iraq. In answer to my question, "Who forged the Niger documents?" Giraldi said, "[A] couple of former CIA officers who are familiar with that part of the world who are associated with a certain well-known neoconservative who has close connections with Italy."[22].

Listen to Horton's Giraldi interview. [23]

---

14.   http://www-cgi.cnn.com/2001/LAW/02/07/embassy.bombing.03/story.fitzgerald.jpg
15.   . http://www.newyorker.com/fact/content/?030512fa_fact
16.   http://antiwar.com/justin/?articleid=6826
17.   http://www.nationalreview.com/ledeen/ledeen200310170840.asp
18.   http://www.washingtonmonthly.com/features/2004/0410.marshallrozen.html
19.   http://64.233.179.104/search?q=cache:HAN49Xf7_g0J:cryptome.org/niger-docs.htm+niger+documents&hl=en
20.   http://www.whitehouse.gov/news/releases/2003/01/20030128-19.html
21.   http://archives.cnn.com/2002/ALLPOLITICS/10/07/bush.transcript/
22.   http://antiwar.com/horton/?articleid=6888 5th paragraph
23.   http://weekendinterviewshow.com/audio/giraldi.mp3

Why was Judith Miller in jail for 85 days? She was making a plea bargain, by basically saying the investigation had to be limited so not to spread on into AIPAC and everything explained below. Libby who based on his little love letter to Miller in jail, I believe has a love interest in her and he cracked under the pressure of her being in jail and gave himself up as a source. It was no shocker. If I could have predicted[24] that he was a source over a year ago then certainly the main stream media with all their resources should have known.

Libby has since been indicted on lesser charges than many people had hoped for and this has caused a wave of Fitzgerald skepticism. Fitzgerald is always two steps ahead of the masses. Libby is a 55 year old man; whether he gets 20 years or 40 years in jail is of no real consolation to him, either way it is life in prison. By using the more air tight lesser charges, Patrick Fitzgerald has cornered Libby without even having to drag it into a larger court battle. Lewis Libby is not a small fish. He was the top man under the Vice President. You could say he was Cheney's Karl Rove. Now, he has resigned—much like Richard Perle, who decided to resign from the DOD right around the same time the FBI raided AIPAC's headquarters for the second time. Some think Perle resigned because Seymour Hersh was pushing for investigation into Perle's possible profiteering. But then the other Israeli firster Douglas Feith also decided to resign. How coincidental!

This investigation, no matter how under reported, is the crack in the Neocons' dam. It will bring the roaches out into the light and expose the OSP and all the LIES they used to foster a war with Iraq as PNAC called for in 1997.

---

24. http://www.rys2sense.com/anti-neocons/viewtopic.php?t=645

27

The Plame affair and the AIPAC spy ring cases are coming together.

David Wurmser, a wormy Zionist who was Cheney's Middle East advisor, is now turning on his fellow Neocons, indicating that senior officials in (Darth) Cheney's office told them to leak information about Plame's CIA identity.[1] This was more than a strike at Wilson this was a power play for the rest of the CIA, saying if you go against us we can blow your covers.

In a piece titled "**Second Cheney aide cooperating in leak probe, those close to case say**" Jason Leopold and Larisa Alexandrovna report:[2]

"Wurmser, Cheney's Middle East advisor and an assistant to then-Under Secretary of State for Arms Control and International Security Affairs John Bolton, likely cooperated because he faced criminal charges for his role in leaking Wilson's name on the orders of higher-ups, the sources said.

According to those familiar with the case, Wurmser was in attendance at several meetings of the White House Iraq Group (WHIG), a little-known cabal of administration hawks that formed in August 2002 to publicize the threat posed by Saddam Hussein. Those who say they have reviewed documents obtained in the probe assert that the Vice President was also present at some of the group's meetings."[3]

"Wurmser's cooperation with Fitzgerald would certainly come as no surprise to those who have been following his career. Last year, he was questioned by the Federal Bureau of Investigation for his possible role in leaking U.S. security secrets to Israel."[4]

---

1. http://rawstory.com/news/2005/
    Second Cheney aide cooperating in leak 1019.html
2. *http://rawstory.com/news/2005/Second Cheney aide cooperating in leak 1019.html*
3. *http://rawstory.com/news/2005/Second Cheney aide cooperating in leak 1019.html*
    3d and 4th paragraph

Oh look at that he TOO is suspected of spying for Israel. Well Maybe he can join AIPAC's Ledeen who worked with the DOD's Larry Franklin to give Rosen and Weissman classified intelligence to pass to Israel. AIPAC is not a lobby group it is a *bribing* group and a *spy* network.

Why is a super Zionist Neocon suddenly cooperating? It is to reduce his own accountability obviously. What is great about the Neocons is they have no loyalty to any one or anything and they will rat on one another.

Now who oh who could be the higher ups that ordered Wurmser to leak this information? I will take a not so wild stab and say it was even higher than Richard Perle and Douglas Feith. Both of these Jewish Israeli firsters decided to resign shortly after the FBI raided AIPAC's head quarters. This thing goes to the very top.[5]

And now look here September 4, 2004 Washington Post,

"*The investigators have asked questions about personnel in the office of Pentagon Undersecretary for Policy Douglas J. Feith as well as members of the influential Defense Policy Board, an advisory panel for Defense Secretary Donald H. Rumsfeld, according to former U.S. officials who have been questioned and others familiar with the case.*

Investigators have specifically asked about a group of neoconservatives involved in defense issues, including Feith, Deputy Defense Secretary Paul D. Wolfowitz, Iraq and Iran specialist Harold Rhode and others at the Pentagon. FBI agents also have asked current and former officials about Richard Perle of the defense board and David Wurmser, an Iran specialist and principal deputy assistant for national security affairs in Cheney's office, according to sources familiar with or involved in the case."[6]

This case with Rove, Miller, Libby, and so on, is linked to another huge scandal in the DOD: The Larry Franklin/AIPAC scandal. Where Israel was using a DOD official to hand over classified information to their lobby group AIPAC who then passed it to the Israeli government. This is not speculation, it is already done, Larry Franklin has pleaded guilty, and he has since gotten 12 years in jail.

---

4.   http://rawstory.com/news/2005/Second_Cheney_aide_cooperating_in_leak_1019.html
      14th paragraph

5.   I gave my predictions of Cheney's involvement on February 10th on KUCI 88.9fm
      Radio http://www.realrepublic.com/userfiles/ry/ryinterview-02–10–06.mp3

6.   *By Robin Wright and Dan Eggen* Washington Post Staff Writers Saturday, September
      4, 2004;   Page   A04   http://www.washingtonpost.com/ac2/wp-dyn/A60497–
      2004Sep3?language=printer

"A former Pentagon analyst who gave classified information to an Israeli diplomat and two members of a pro-Israel lobbying group was sentenced Friday to more than 12 years in prison. Lawrence A. Franklin, a policy analyst whose expertise included Iraq and Iran, pleaded guilty in October to three felony counts. Three other counts were dropped as part of the plea deal"[7]

SO Larry Franklin the spy in the DOD who gave AIPAC top secret documents about Iran, has been given over 12 years in jail![8]

The case is widening. Steve Rosen[9] and Keith Weissman[10] the AIPAC officials, who were fired, have both been indicted and are set to go on trial in August[11]. Israel's dirty spy ring is being uncovered and it is deeply composed of people in the Office of Special Plans. Everything connects as pointed out in this thread.[12]

Two senior employees of the American Israel Public Affairs Committee, one of Washington's most influential lobbying organizations, have left their jobs amid an FBI investigation into whether they passed classified U.S. information to the government of Israel, a source close to the organization said yesterday.[13]

(The Washington post is too kind in using the words "left their jobs".)

But let me put something together. At first one may think that the reason for ousting Plame was because she or one of her fellow agents working for the same CIA front company could determine who forged the Niger uranium claims documents. This was **a** reason however it is much bigger than that! The Documents that Franklin passed to AIPAC who passed it to Israel were stolen to gather a case for war with Iran. The scare tactic that the neocons are using is a claim that Iran is building nuclear weapons. Ousting Plame and BJA undermined our ability to track nuclear weapons proliferation. Thus it made a fog of war over the case on Iran's nuclear capacity, from which they can launch their propaganda. Iran does not have a bomb, but our old clandestine methods of assuring that have been lost

7.   http://www.cbsnews.com/stories/2006/01/20/national/main1224809.shtml
8.   http://www.cbsnews.com/stories/2006/01/20/national/main1224809.shtml
9.   AIPAC's policy director who has since been fired and indicted.
10. AIPAC's Iran specialist who has since been fired and indicted.
11. This trial has since been moved to May 25th 2006
12. http://www.rys2sense.com/anti-neocons/viewtopic.php?t=645
13. http://www.washingtonpost.com/wp-dyn/articles/A6059-2005Apr20.html

with the Plame Affair. Does anyone still question that we went to war for Israel and that Israel is directing us to war for them again?

28

Why hasn't this scandal been major news?

This is going to tear apart the neocons! I hope we can stall the war against Iran the AIPAC trial when this nasty cabal will finally be revealed in public courts.

Interestingly, the Israeli spy ring this time through AIPAC (not the ADL for once) dates back before September 11 2001 where Mossad agents were living next door to the patsies/terrorists (depending on your view of that). Could this be the work of a foreign intelligence operation?—YES! Israel has a history of false flag operations starting from the 1950s to today

The OSP lied us into the war, and the OSP is Zionist. We know that the OSP was spying on the US for Israel, because PNAC was based on Israeli policy papers from 1996. PNAC called for a war with Iraq and for a Pearl Harbor as an event to justify it. We know that, too. 911 was an inside job. Franklin's boss Richard Perle was caught spying for Israel before. Indeed, the FBI has gag orders on people (Sible Edmonds) relating to transcripts from Perle and his goons admitting prior knowledge. Israel had Mossad agents caught on 911 in a white van who worked for a fake moving company in Jersey. Connect the dots, people! WE WENT TO WAR FOR ISRAEL. 911 was planned and carried out by a faction from Israel and their moles are in our own government, who are supported by the Christian fanatics who profiteer from it. They are living on a Straussian theology (I will not even call it an ideology).

God damn, we have a foreign government spying on the US who has openly stated they wanted war with Iraq in PNAC and who has undermined our ability to track nuclear weapons by ousting Valerie Plame (and her front company), something this same fascist country did before with their spy Jonathon Pollard. On top of that, the documents they stole in the spying all pertain to gathering intelligence on Iran and how to best to construct a case for war. This is not the illuminati or the Vatican, or as one particular nut ball is claiming, the space lizards, etc. It is not the free-masons, and it is not a cult of Satan worshipers, it is the Zionists plain and simple, and there is plenty of clear evidence for it.

PNAC was first written in Israel. It was chiefly composed by Paul Wolfowitz, Richard Perle, Lewis Libby, Douglas Feith, Bill Kristal (CFR)[1] and Elliot Abrams (CFR) Aaron Friedberg also (CFR) Donald Kagan (CFR) and Stephen Rosen (the AIPAC employee caught spying on the US!!) they all Zionists and all Jewish. That's not anti-Semitic it's just the truth and all Jewish. Why does being Jewish even matter? Because it means they have dual citizenship to Israel. Because of the Law of return[2] all US Jews are automatically granted citizenship with Israel. Wolfowitz lived there until his teens and currently has a sister living there. They put Israel's interests above America's interests. It would be a mathematical impossibility for such a small portion of America's population to have such lopsided representation in the civilian, (non-elected) portion of the government if something else was not going on.

We got the facts folks we don't need to dive into secret occult societies. We can see where the contracts are going and where the oil is going and it isn't to the Vatican or some amorphous secret group. It's to Israel and the profiteers in the US in the MIC. Haliburton-KBR was an old LBJ favorite.

> *"The story of Halliburton's ties to the White House dates back to the 1940s, when a Texas firm called Brown & Root constructed a massive dam project near Austin. The company's founders, Herman and George Brown, won the contract to build Mansfield Dam thanks to the efforts of Johnson, who was then a Texas congressman.*
>
> *After Johnson took over the Oval Office, Brown & Root won contracts for huge construction projects for the federal government. By the mid-1960s, newspaper columnists and the Republican minority in Congress began to suggest that the company's good luck was tied to its sizable contributions to Johnson's political campaign.*

More questions were raised when a consortium of which Brown & Root was a part won a $380 million contract to build airports, bases, hospitals and other facilities for the U.S. Navy in South Vietnam. By 1967, the General Accounting Office had faulted the *"Vietnam builders"*—as they were known—for massive accounting lapses and allowing thefts of materials."[3]

---

1.   Council of Foreign Relations
2.   http://www.jewishvirtuallibrary.org/jsource/Immigration/
       Text_of_Law_of_Return.html
3.   http://www.npr.org/templates/story/story.php?storyId=1569483

Yes, this is the same Lyndon B. Johnson who told the US to stand down and allow the attack on the USS Liberty by the Israelis. He was screaming over the phone that he wanted "...that god damn ship going to the bottom." This is the same LBJ who was, in my opinion, deeply involved in the JFK and RFK assassinations. But that could be an entirely different book. The Warren Commission has a lot in common with the 911 commission. Needless to say, Israel enjoyed a cozy relationship with LBJ and served the interests of the MIC fifty years ago over both Israel and America's best interests.

Think about what Bush's father was doing at this time in his eventual rise to the head of the CIA then Vice president and then president. It started under LBJ's wing. Note that these same crazies were cooking up such insanities as Operation Northwoods. The CIA/Mossad operates like the old East India Tea Company did for England. They serve like giant corporate factions which can effectively act like shadow governments. The People that the Reagan administration called, "the crazies in the basement" are back, they have always been around, they have always been Zionists and religious nuts, and they are on full throttle today. As the Neocons get backed into a corner from the different court cases, you can bet that Israel will try to jump start the rest of the Clean Break Strategy by bunking up some reason to attack Palestine, Lebanon and Syria. When they hit Syria, Iran will be pulled in and the US will with its Zionists masters in Israel, be starting WWIII which could spill into Russia, China, and maybe even Japan and North Korea.

People it's ISRAEL not the illuminati, not the Vatican, and certainly not the space lizards. It's ISRAEL who is the force here behind these Zionists Neocons taking us to war. There is a crowd of people I must address so if this doesn't pertain to you then pay it no mind. Stop promoting the asinine propaganda you hear from Protestant Christian radio programs which are utterly blind to reality and waste time chasing satanic cults and Babylonian deities and start talking about real evidence and real people who are driving us into war. It takes about three seconds to look at the proposed structures of the supposed 'illuminati' and see it is made up of old catholic military orders like the knights of templar and so forth who have absolutely nothing to do with the war in Iraq, the coming war with Lebanon, Syria and Iran, or 911. Protestant extremists want to shuck the crimes of Christianity on to the Catholics and claim that they worship the Devil (i.e. they are not real Christians) because they want to escape their own historical responsibility of their own mass murders and atrocities.

The Catholic Church is guilty of enough of its own real crimes from genocide to pedophilia, without having to invent any extras. However, it is the Protestant Churches who have the strong alliance with the fascist state of Israel. They give more money to Israel than anyone else. Go read anti-neocons.com and get some sane news that doesn't talk about secret satanic hand signals akin to the Texas Longhorns sign or the deaf sign for "I love you." Above all please stop talking about the spooky junk on the one dollar bill. Most junk on the current dollar bill came from 1956 when Republicans took control of both houses. It was not set up by our forefathers. On Anti-neocons.com we report factual things untainted by Protestant baloney.

Here is a question you may have asked yourself. If 911 was an inside job, then why was there so much prior knowledge of the attacks? Granted it was ignored, but how could there be intelligence of an Al Qaeda ring in the US and all those pilots going to flight schools, and the warning about Bin Laden wanting to attack America, if the said hijackers didn't do it which is irrefutably evident by the fact that some of them are alive? That's right, Saeed Al-Ghamdi, Mohand Al-Shehri, Abdul Aziz Al-Omari and Salem Al-Hazmi are not dead.[4] Just where did the list of the infamous 19 hijackers come from anyway?

Why risk them getting busted if they were patsies? Since the hijackers didn't do it how was there any evidence of them planning an attack that they didn't do and obviously didn't even know about considering they were going to get the blame? Furthermore if the government really did 911 then why leak information about your own patsies and look like incompetent fools when the warnings were ignored?

The prior knowledge arguments do have evidence. They do two things. They make the Bush administration look incompetent for not acting on supplied information and they make it look like the attacks could have been prevented had Bush and company only read the memos they were being given. What that does is make it appear like the attack was done by Arab terrorists. The Democrats naturally jumped all over this. It was a chance to make Republicans look bad yet still blame 911 on Arab terrorists.

Someone was dropping hints and information to imply that the terrorists were Arabs and mainly from Saudi Arabia. Why did they frame Saudi Arabia if it was a frame and they were patsies then why not use at least one Iraqi after all that is who they wanted to attack and did attack after 911. Why Saudi Arabia? What's

---

4.   http://news.bbc.co.uk/1/hi/world/middle_east/1559151.stm

with all the seeds about Saudi Arabia planted by the Leftwing of the Neocon monster?

The answer is clear when you understand who really carried out 911, the Israeli Mossad and their Neocon moles and their blackmail controlled shills. Someone obviously wanted to pin the 911 terrorists' attacks on Muslim Arabs. Someone has tried this multiple times in the past with the USS Liberty attack, the Lavon Affair/Operation Susanna. And we know when Israel did this they had the complicity of the US president who illegitimately was put into power by some faction who murdered the president.

One of the most laughable parts of the 911 story was the FBI finding Atta's unburned passport at ground zero. Yes, they want us to believe that a paper passport which can fit in a person's pocket, was found at ground zero (amidst all the rubble) miraculously escaping a fireball and inferno that allegedly defied the laws of physics and was hot enough to bring down two sky scrapers and leave molten steel (from the thermate) at the base. What a crock. Atta's passport had been reported stolen in 1999. Magically that same missing and stolen passport was the one found at ground zero. Geee someone must have put it there for the FBI to find in order to implicate Muslim Arab terrorists.

Could it get any worse? Yes it can. Mohammed Atta supposedly went to Portland Maine just before the attacks where he simply left a bag full of incriminating information such as a hijackers manual, (whatever that is) and a list of the 19 hijackers! This is clearly planted evidence. But who put it there?

Well let's take a look at the flight school in Florida where Atta was training. Rudi Dekkers was Atta's (or someone pretending to be Atta's) flight instructor in Florida. Note that we know that the Israeli Mossad was living next door[5] to Atta in Florida (supposedly monitoring him). In fact the BBC reported[6] that yet another Israel spy-ring was operation in the US prior to 911 with over 120 agents. Der Spiegel reported about the "Israeli Art Students" who had been infiltrating federal offices and living next to the so called hijackers.

> *"An entire troop of Israeli terror investigators disguised as students took to the tracks of Arabic terrorists and their cells in the USA between December 2000 and April 2001. During their undercover investigations, the Israelis came very close to the later perpetrators of September 11. In Hollywood, Florida they located both of the former Hamburg students and later terrorist pilots Mohammed Atta and Marwan al-Shehhi as potential terrorists. Agents settled down in immediate proximity*

---

5.   http://www.antiwar.com/justin/j100402.html
6.   http://news.bbc.co.uk/1/hi/world/europe/2294487.stm

of their apartment and observed the seemingly normal flight school students around the clock. [7]

Well Mohammed Atta, the same guy whose passport was found at ground zero and who conveniently left the FBI a bag full of incriminating evidence, went to a flight school in Florida. Now Rudi Dekkers, his flight school instructor, discovered that Atta could not speak German. It's well known that Mohammed Atta lived in Hamburg Germany, yet suddenly he must have forgotten how to speak German. Dekkers a Dutch citizen tried to converse with Atta who stared at him and had to ignore him eventually making a point that he was leaving for Boston. Ha even the Mossad could not anticipate that one, the flight instructor in Florida was fluent in German and almost ruined their patsy. Similarly, Zacharias Moussaoui, reportedly couldn't understand French. [8] The Following has been reported on here, this person would like to remain anonymous for safety concerns but the work is in the footnote after the quote..

> *"The real Atta would have been able to respond to his instructor's German small talk and the real Moussaoui would have been able to respond to his instructor's French small talk."* [9]

I must agree the REAL Atta and Moussaoui, could have responded. Well SOMEBODY was trying to create information about Arab Hijackers training for 911. SOMEBODY was living next to their partner Atta-bizzaro. No wonder Atta was seen so many times on the casino ships with Jack Abramoff. Yes, Atta was spotted on the Zionist criminal Jack Abramoff's SunCruz Casino ships in Florida on September 5th 2001 six days before 911!! [10] What on earth was he doing there meeting with a Zionists crook who has been busted in a plethora of scandals involving our congress? He was not Atta he was the Mossad's own boy. They killed the real Atta. Then they took his stolen passport and planted the evidence for the FBI to find. The other hijackers also had there passports stolen. It does not take a genius to figure out who did that and why. SOMEBODY left his passport at ground zero and then SOMEBODY wrote letters for the anthrax attacks steering Americas rage on to Israel's enemies.

7.   http://www.spiegel.de/politik/ausland/0,1518,216421,00.html
8.   http://www.prisonplanet.com/
      eagan_flight_trainer_wouldnt_let_unease_about_moussaoui_rest.html
9.   http://www.apfn.org/apfn/WTC_STF.htm
10.   http://en.wikipedia.org/wiki/Mohammed_Atta (scroll down to September 05)

Shortly after 911 we had two different Anthrax letters trying to blame 911 on the Arabs. One read:

"You cannot stop us. We have this anthrax. You die now. Are you afraid? Death to America. Death to Israel. Allah is great."

And the other read: *"This is next. Take Penacilin now. Death to America. Death to Israel. Allah is great."*

Death to America and Death to Israel...Gee I wonder who really wrote that. Might it be Israel? SOMEONE wants to say Bid Laden is in Afghanistan (he is dead by the way) Al Qeada is in Iraq, Anthrax came from Egypt, and 911 came from Saudi Arabia, and Iran is making a nuclear bomb. SOMEBODY is full of it and has been caught in their lies and deceptions in the past and present despite the Main Stream Media Black out. SOMEBODY wants a war not against terrorists but against Israel's enemies (AKA the rouge nations, the few countries left on the planet that don't have privately owned central banks.)

Who could that be? Who got caught on 911 in a white van that had traces of explosives in it and worked for a moving company which turned out to be a front for the Israeli Mossad? 5 Israeli agents got caught and the first thing out of their mouths was:

"We are Israelis. We are not your problem. Your problems are our problems. The Palestinians are your problem."

Gosh, English speaking, x-military, explosives experts, cheering and taking pictures of the WTC burning towers in NY on 911, who worked for a fake moving company which was a front for the Mossad, driving a van that had a hit with bomb sniffing dogs, and over 4.5 thousand dollars stuffed in a sock, is nothing to be concerned about. Sivan Kurzberg could still say with a straight face. 'It wasn't me, blame the Palestinians.'

The picture is coming more clear. But don't blame it all on Israel. I focus on this wing of it because it is the most unmentioned part about the 911 story because people in the alternative press are too afraid of the ADL and knee jerk Liberals calling them anti-Semites. They aren't ALL Jewish or Ashka*nazis* as a better name may be, they aren't even all Zionists aside from when it temporarily serves their own interest. People like Daryle Bradford Smith have been mentioning the Zionist side of thing but giving a pass to the Christian Zionists and the corporatists. I know the guy is not an anti-Semite but still the Jewishness of it only goes so far. Loosely calling people crypto Jews is not helping anything. (Likewise there are other people who really are Anti-Semites like Neo-nazi groups who are blaming the Jews for everything including WWII and anything else bad in history). There are plenty of Oil executives who were in on this that don't give a damn about Israel or the Jews, they just have overlapping interests with the Zionists on Iraq as they wanted to get Saddam out for selling too much oil and therefore lowering the price per barrel. And they are ignoring the Sherman Anti-trust laws by granting OPEC more of a monopoly on oil. They are bottlenecking it on purpose to increase the price and they are making hundreds of millions from it personally. But the oil tycoons could not get away with this in the press if were it not serving a Zionist end because that is who undoubtedly controls the media. Just look at the non-coverage of the Israeli occupation of Palestine as one flagrant example.

So we have a nasty team-up here each codependent on the other. They are using one another. Oil executives however rich, are not a country, they do not have the power and capabilities to create such false flag operations and infiltrate the US government with hundreds of spies and moles like Israel has. Next on Israel's check list are Hezbollah, Lebanon, and Syria. Israel will have no trouble massacring civilians and spinning it as defense against terrorism. In truth they are the terrorists and the US will undoubtedly ignore reality and support Israel unconditionally. When gas goes to $100 a barrel and the dollars has its purchasing power diminished, you will wish you had spoken out against Israel's fascist plans. Another war is coming and the US will, regardless of public opinion and outcry, been over backwards and suck its thumb for Israel. The US government was part of this, I am certain Cheney knows everything. He personally had NORAD stand down. The Mossad could do the rest. This next election it is time to clean up congress. If we are lucky and Israel doesn't start WWIII this Summer, we can knock out every incumbent who has a race this November. Don't vote based on parties. Vote based on this single most important thing, are they pro-war or anti-war? Take America back this November. NO MORE WAR FOR ISRAEL!

29

Breaking down the reasons for the Iraq war

—**Why was there really a war?** The 911 links to Iraq were a myth. The WMD were a myth. The charges about uranium were out right lies. Spreading democracy is a joke, as it is we don't even have fair elections here and there is no way it will happen in Iraq. So why the hell did we go there? It would be absurd to say there was just a single reason for the war; a breakdown of the reasons is warranted.

Oil?

Operation Iraqi Liberation, spelled OIL, is one popular reason, but this is not the main reason. Corporate profiteering is at an all time high, and there is no corporation as large as the military industrial complex. Even the bloated pentagon budget and pork projects for lobbyist PACs and cabinet members are not the main reason for the war. All these things were extra incentives for the crooks that run our government but not the main reason for the war.

Iron Triangle?

The stock market allows for a whole new loophole, a whole new concrete method for the ties between big business and government. All a politician has to do is pass legislation favorable to the companies s/he has stock in or works for to gain huge profits. This has made our government up for rent. Any war would work for this end, even a cold war. Why Iraq?

The United States' unconditional support of Israel's fascist police state?

If you really want to stop terrorism then we need to stop financing the Zionist bigots in Israel, who are using US weapons, ironically named after American

Indians[1], to do to people exactly what the US did to the Indians, which was the greatest crime in all of history. Here, in the US, we don't study history, we rationalize it, or sometimes we just lie about it. I wonder if, in the future, we will have Gaza submarines or Jenin jets.

Israel receives around ten million dollars a day from the United States. Most people do not know this and if they did, considering the current state of the economy and the unethical uses of the money, I am sure they would not want it sent there.

So, what are the real reasons for this war, and the sending of this money? Answering this question is easy, all one has to do is look at who will profit the most and who orchestrated it—ChristioZionist fanatics and big business.

The weapons industry is a business and like any other giant US corporation they are corrupt and care nothing about human rights or public welfare, they only care about profits. This is not simply a problem with accounting or confused CEOs. This is a problem with purposefully immoral people who have realized that the American judicial system often places money over ethics. We are all suffering from the greed of upper class America. No industry is as dangerous as the weapons industry, because they are in the business of killing. A protracted war benefits arms and energy companies.

The anti-occupation forces in Iraq will never stop, and why should they? This war is not winnable short of genocide. There is no legitimate reason for the US to be occupying another country. People should be in jail for the lies which have led to the death of 100,000 Iraqi civilians, billions of dollars, and over 2,066 American lives.

Our fat cats get fatter and the religious flocks and blind patriots continue to support them because the only information they can get on the war is from our Zionist-owned media. Large corporations who do not give a damn about humanity or freedom run our country.

There have always been people for and against war throughout history. A deeper question might be how do we ever convince thousands of absolute strangers to go kill each other? It is one thing to be attacked like Crazy Horse was attacked by Custer and he defeated him. What about the people who are attacking? Why did they risk their lives and for what?

It is nothing more than a combination of greed and manipulation. Then there is that ever present need for vicarious masculinity, which the "chicken hawks" feed on daily. The State becomes an extension of their ego. The war party takes

---

1.   (Tomahawk cruise missiles, Blackhawk, Apache helicopters).

glee in saying they will kick our enemies' asses. "Ah we should just 'nuke them, or "make a glass parking lot". I have actually heard these phrases spoken by grown adults. Not stupid people either. I mean business men who just get frustrated and want that oh so quick and satisfying answer of blowing the hell out of people, you know, showing them who "is boss". I blame that on authoritarianism, but also we need to separate intelligence from compassion. A person can be smart but have the moral compass of a Nazi. The insecurities manifested in numerous ways have gotten many people; both smart and dumb, to have a greater need for an ego boost than for a caring relationship for humanity and the planet. Caring is considered 'weak.'

Western science and religions have both made a clean break with and a war on relationships with nature. The endless pursuit of shiny things, i.e. status through ownership, has led to a nation of islands. No-one sees that personal comforts and private interests cannot be a blindfold to our relationship to world events and changes in our environment. But, the head in the sand apathy is allowing a minority of evil people, evolutionarily parasites, to gather the sheep for battle, as they get off on their wargasm.

People don't think of what is just and then act. They act, and then think of how to justify it. Greed and envy will rationalize everything. Another part of the puzzle is that war has become distant. Technology allows the horror of war to be separated by machines from the individual. It's easier to drop a bomb than to run in and get blood on your hands. It's becoming game like.

On the bright side, man has evolved in some areas. Northern Europe, for example and many of the island nations are not going to war on their own without US manipulation. As long as we have a culture that bases its human worth on occupational income and property, we are going to hell. Yes, property has become a method of gaining status with others and with one's self. What we need is a value system that places prestige in compassion, intelligence, creativity, and actual aspects of character rather than on material gain and ability to take from others.

30

War and the support of the Christian Reich-(Right) Divorcing Morality from Religion

o o o o o o o o o o o o o o o o o o o o o o o o o o o o o o o o o o

"Those who can make you believe absurdities can make you commit atrocities."

—*Voltaire*

Moderate Christians should be up in arms at the fringe elements of Christianity; they have got to be the biggest turn off to their faith in existence. **I'd like to thank the Presbyterian church for their divestment from Israel**[1]. History will always record you as the first to take this critical step for humanity. If the Episcopal/Anglocan[2] church will follow the divestment[3] it could restore my faith in humanity. We all know the Born-Agains will never do this; they are a religion of division and hatred which often preys upon addicts and the abused.

"Morality and religion have become so intertwined that many people cannot conceive of ethics divorced from god, even in principle."[4] Religious people have a disastrous way of thinking that pits a world view where without religion everything is cultural relativism, which is further twisted to mean that there is no such thing as right and wrong. They believe that only through religious teachings can

---

1. http://www.here-now.org/shows/2004/07/20040716_3.asp
2. http://www.beliefnet.com/story/153/story_15369_1.html
3. http://www.beliefnet.com/story/155/story_15507_1.html
4. Paragraph 6, VII. The Significance of Atheism. http://www.positiveatheism.org/writ/smith.htm

societies have a clear cut basis for right and wrong (never mind basing it on reason).

First of all, even if things were just cultural relativism that would not mean that right and wrong did not exist, it would mean that some rights and wrongs would be different in different cultures. And even within these there would be truths with in a paradigm.* Kant, Hume, Mills, and others found ways and systems around cultural relativism, each in a unique way but never mind that for now.

It is a terrible mistake to equate religion with morality. For one, religion has the worst track record for organizing human beings into committing atrocities. The Bible, for example, supports the divine right of kings, an authoritarian form of government prone to war and corruption. In Christianity's peek of political power, people lived under kings where 90% of the population were serfs. Slavery is supported and advocated in the bible so is animal sacrifice, as well as the second rate status of women and a slew of other ills. Now apologists (rationalization makers) will claim that the Christians of the past, who pretty much had nonstop war, inquisitions, genocide of American Indians under manifest destiny, burned young women believing them to be witches and threw scientist in jail for saying things we now believe to be true, were not REAL Christians. This is just not true. The entire concept of witches, divine kings, and killing heretics can not exist without the religion.

There are also more minor sexual and dietary taboos invented by religion. The few good concepts like don't steal and don't kill people can be understood by a four year old and hardly warrants a belief in a god or a religious text to understand them. But even these simple moral values that a toddler can understand are broken by religious people with flimsy excuses. Murder is OK if it is a war, and war is OK if it's for your religion. Who has stolen from and murdered more people than Christians?

More Jews have been killed by Christians than by Muslims or any other people. More Muslims have been killed by Christians than by anyone else. More Native Americans have been killed by Christians namely Catholics, than by anyone else. More Africans have been killed by Christians than by anyone else. More Christians have been killed by other Christians than by anyone else. More land has been stolen by Christians than by anyone else. In fact the Pope once arrogantly divided all of the new-world between Portugal and Spain.

There are some forms of Christianity, that take the good principles more seriously, like the Quakers who believe in non violence, yet according to Ben Franklin, did not have trouble provoking violence from Native Americans by swindling them in business deals and then allowing others to defend them.

What makes a person moral, is integrity, compassion, and intelligence (all innate human characteristics). Authoritative systems do not foster these attributes, they cater to fear and place virtue and love in obedience not knowledge.

Our founding fathers many of them atheist and desist broke away from religion and the systems set up by such belief systems. The whole concept of a republic, as opposed to divine rule, was a step away from religious absolutism. Freedom and democracy are not Biblical principles. The Bible has King David, King Solomon, and King Saul. There is no voting in the Bible.

Religion serves as authoritative sources to justify crimes against humanity. You don't need a god to believe killing stealing and lying are wrong. Two of the Ten Commandments mention **slavery** and nowhere does it mention slavery is immoral and wrong. The fourth commandment mentions that even slaves don't have to work on the Sabbath day. And the Tenth commandment says for men not to covet their neighbor's oxen, wife, or slaves. Some revisionist Bibles now say maidservants in place of the word slaves. They can change the words but we have close to two thousand years of recorded history showing they damn well meant and practiced slavery.

It is simply insane to say that religious philosophy is a good ground work for moral values. It creates clear and rigid prejudices. Members of the faith can not even allow themselves to THINK differently under the threat of force, actually under the threat of eternal punishment.

Who currently has such a problem with homosexuals? Religious people. Who is it that blindly supports a war based on lies and has thus supported killing hundreds of thousands of Iraqis? Religious people. Who has an on going conflict between Zionist Jews and Palestinians (or really any non-Zionist)? Religious people. Northern Ireland…Religious people. Muslims and Hindu fighting in Kashmir, religious people again. Who has a fit about stem cell research and abortions?- Religious people. Actually all of these are a mixture of Religion and politics. This is why it is crucial to keep religion out of politics. Be a foolish hate filled bigot on your own time but keep it out of the government!

It's not that religion is intrinsically evil—far from it. Some of the leading anti-war champions are Christian, George Galloway, David Ray Griffin, Alex Jones, Dennis Kucinich, and Scott Ritter to name a few. And of course there are anti-war Atheist, Justin Raimondo, Bill Maher, and Jon Stewart and so on.

Religion is like a car, it is the driver that really matters, and under a good or greedy culture the same religion can be used entirely differently. That still doesn't change my opinion of the trueness of religions; the public ones are clearly man-made fictions and the personal ones are by their nature, private, so there would be no way to make a judgment about them.

What is verifiable is that the major religious <u>institutions</u> in the United States historically and currently have financed the worst crimes of our country. They are assisting the occupation in Israel with money and rhetoric, and they invest in the war machine in Iraq. It is not to color all Christians by the lunatic ravings of Jerry Falwell and Pat Robertson who call for political assassinations, and blame 911 on gay people. These men, under any other context than religion, would be declared insane. But people need to realize that the extremist of their own faith cannot just be brushed aside. Something deeper is going on here. If the majority of Christians were able to see these evangelicals as none other than angry money grubbing bigots (which some are), then why do these loud hate fill bastards have so much voice?

It is because they back the government. They are part of the embedded media. The government can turn something golden into absolute manure. And that is what we have here, 'HypoChristianity'. This is why everyone, atheist and religious alike, should want their government as far away as possible from religion. We need more moderate Christians to make a stand. We need more moderate Jews, Muslims, etc to take a hard stand against the extremist of their own faiths. Pat Robertson is nothing more than a Christian version of Usama Bin Laden. The Christian-Reich has too much power. What about a rise of say the Christian left? It could join with secular voices maybe not on opinions on theology but on common support for humanity.

31

Connecting the dots makes a star

"*Battalion Seven Chief: "Battalion Seven…Ladder 15, we've got two isolated pockets of fire. We should be able to knock it down with two lines. Radio that, 78th floor numerous 10–45 Code Ones."*[1] *NYCFD tapes.* (The fires in one tower were almost out they thought they could put it down with two lines, that was before the bombs went off.)

Many people are now saying that 911 was an inside job. A few years ago this kind of talk would get you labeled crazy. I have been saying it from almost the beginning. What really tipped me off though was George Bush claiming he saw the first plane hit live on TV before he went into the school room in Florida to read with people above his reading level. This was impossible because there was no footage of the first plane hitting until well after September 11th. Naturally the main 'spin' media ignored this story. That's OK at least we have the web. Type in this footnote on your PC and watch it yourself.[2]

In the beginning I had my questions about 911, especially the building that fell down at 5pm, because to me it was common sense that it was a demolition. Within days when I saw the Anthrax letters, I knew what was really going on. But deep down I did not want to admit it. I knew what was true, but I had not psychologically digested it yet. After Bush told this boldface lie and the press didn't question it, the scales fell from my eyes. It got bigger as we went to war with Iraq, and it became more and more obvious that this was not just our foul government at work but a nasty little foreign power as well.

Most of the "911 was an inside job" camps like to lay out 4 scenarios about what happened. Briefly they go as follows:

---

1.   http://www.thememoryhole.org/911/firefighter-tape-excerpts.htm
2.   http://www.whatreallyhappened.com/IMAGES/bushsawfirstplane1.ram

1 **Is the official story.**
We got caught with our pants down and terrorists did 911. And the wars in the Middle East are part of the greater war on terrorism.

2 **The incompetence excuse**
There was information available about the coming attacks but because of our incompetence we failed to see it. Terrorists attacked the US. And the wars in the Middle East were based on mistakes (more incompetence) but now we have got to stay there.

3 **They let it happen**
They knew full well about the coming 911 attacks but allowed it to happen in order to use it as a pretext to go to war with Iraq and Afghanistan as it was in military and corporate interests (particularly oil) to do so.

4 **They made it happen**. (*They* meaning just vaguely the Bush Administration)
The Bush government either helped protect the terrorists or simply used them as patsies, and assisted the plane crashes effects with bombs placed inside the towers prior to 911. The wars in the Middle East were about oil.

The "911 was an inside job" camps then say that the evidence must land you somewhere between scenarios 3 and 4 with more research dropping you firmly on number 4.

Let me now throw in a 5th scenario.
5 **The Neocons Made it happen with the assistance of a foreign government**, the same government where PNAC was first written, and who we have caught spies from who have been stealing secrets from us about Iran, and who made up the shadow government of the OSP which is who cherry picked and fabricated the lies told about Iraq in order to start the war. The Wars in the Middle East were for separate reasons, Afghanistan was about a few pipelines as noted but more so about controlling large quantities of un-tapped uranium (a reason for both the Russian and US invasions) and secondly for controlling opium as the CIA uses drug money to fund its off the books black operations such as the now known massive secret prison systems and torture camps. Also coupled with that are the various color coded revolutions which aim to circle China and Russia with US bases, (add to that the lesser known negotiations with Japan to allow nuclear subs into the Japanese Sea [pointed at China] in exchange for moving troops

from Okinawa to Guam and indirect LDP funding). The main goal, however, which PNAC states, is to keep the eye on the pie~Iran (which Afghanistan and Iraq both boarder.) The invasion of Iraq was to solve Israel's oil crisis and stop the threat of a secular Middle East which would become a true economic player and was a threat to the aggressive state of Israel.

The evidence, if it was ALL being stated, especially pertaining to the war in Iraq, would land you somewhere between scenario 4 and 5 and more research would land you firmly in 5.

A lot of films have shown the problems with official 911 fables. There is the demolition of building number 7, which the 911 commission decided to just ignore because they could not explain it, there are the firemen's reports that the fires were almost out, there are numerous reports of secondary explosions etc. Because it has been said on radio and maybe more so because people have made films about it, many people can recite the arguments for the inside job in their sleep. But what has been hidden from you and the dots which have not been connected in any 911 films is the Israeli connection. 911 was an inside job which was part of a larger plan for perpetual war hatched in Israel. 911 and the wars in the Middle East were carefully planned attacks carried out by a faction of Zionist Neocons and the Israeli Mossad. We will start with PNAC and then jump and work backwards from the Iraq War to 911.

A lot of people know about PNAC, but very few people have taken a hard look at its origins. PNAC was co-authored by the same people who've been caught lying about the Iraq War's pre-invasion intelligence. We are talking about only 25 people who helped fabricate evidence and pass it off to the president and journalists. PNAC stems from Israeli policy papers. Now there is a big difference between who actually WROTE PNAC's papers and who just SIGNED them. The Trotskyite neocon slime ball William Kristol was on Colbert Report of all places and explained how Rumsfeld and others were not part of PNAC, "they signed some of our letters," he said but they are not part of the real cabal. Leave it to fake news to get at the real news, it was the first time I have seen Steven Colbert speechless. He must have been biting his tongue not being able to say what he probably wanted to say given that little revelation. The war in Iraq and control over energy resources is all lined out in Israel's A Clean Break: A New Strategy for Securing the Realm[3] "and in both 1992 and 1998 this document was regurgitated as PNAC's letters, written by the same people. Paul Wolfowitz presented the PNAC's open letter[4] to Bill Clinton on January 26, 1998 where the opening

---

3.   http://www.iasps.org/strat1.htm

lines clearly state the desire to go to war with Iraq. "Wolfowitz urged Clinton to recognize a provisional [Iraqi] government headed by the INC[5] under Chalabi."[6] Wow sound familiar?

Later in 2000 PNAC released what is normally referred to the document more of you are familiar with which is commonly but mistakenly just called "PNAC" and that was PNAC's paper, "Rebuilding America's Defenses: Strategies, Forces and Resources for a New Century"[7] This is the paper stating the infamous lines about the need for a New Pearl Harbor...Page 63. The bulk of the document however is about going to war with Iraq. It was a must have to start global new world order.

Now Wolfowitz did not do this on his own, Lewis Libby, Douglas Feith and Richard Perle and others who have recently resigned and are or have been caught up in criminal activity in the past, helped. Interestingly, Perle and Wolfowitz both worked as aides to senator Henry "Swoop" Jackson (A Democrat!). In 1970, while working for Jackson Perle was charged with two heinous acts, spying for the state of Israel and leaking information about the CIA in regards to its nuclear deterrent program, to Russia. Wow! sound familiar?

In the run up to the war in Iraq, there was a lot of disinformation. Once again most people know what that package of lies was about...the mushroom cloud scare tactics, liberating the Kurds, and lastly the joke of democracy building, which have all been shown to be falsehoods or failures.

What people do not seem to know is who made these fabrications. They assume it was just "Bush" and the vague term "the administration". Well yes it was people in the administration, but whom? Well let's break it down. The second most important scandal in the administration which is currently on trial with a second date set for Jan 07, is the Plame outing and Niger forgeries.

Born Again Bush and his Zionists handlers like to blame shift the responsibility of the WMDs myths to the CIA. Well as evil and corrupt as the CIA is, it is not that sloppy. Bush did not just get "mistaken intelligence" or make "miscalculations" he explicitly asked for fabrications.

Here is we have concrete proof that they lied. One of Bush's claims about Iraq was that Saddam was trying to acquire yellow cake uranium from Africa. This rhetoric was further laced in fear by Neo-condelsleeza Rice saying we could not let the smoking gun be a mushroom cloud. What outrageous audacity, (they are

4. http://www.newamericancentury.org/iraqclintonletter.htm
5. Iraqi National Congress
6. http://en.wikipedia.org/wiki/Paul_Wolfowitz
7. http://www.newamericancentury.org/RebuildingAmericasDefenses.pdf

even re-using the same fear-mongering excuses to attack Iran). This could be an air tight case for impeachment if there was an actual opposition party. The Niger forgeries are something you should write your representatives about (if you are an American, otherwise encourage Americans you know to do this). They were so sloppy, and if we had a functional media, Bush and co would be dead in the water. Allele Elhadj Habibou was not even in power at the time of the supposed signature, oops! Now that must be embarrassing.

It would be nice if the mainstream media would report that. Now are you ready to get pulled out of the rabbit hole some more? What did these guys (Ahmad Chalabi, Francis Brookes, Dewey Clarridge, and **Michael Ledeen**.) have to do with the forgeries? Why is it always the same small cabal, the same short list of nasty characters, who always seem to be behind every lie? Could the people who we **know** lied about Iraq also be behind the false flag attack of 911? They wrote about wanting it and then benefited from it, so it is worth taking a look.

Andreas von Bulow the former Defense Minister of Germany said on April 21, 2006[8] on the Alex Jones show that this false flag operation had to be carried out by a very small group of people. Alex asked him "would you say 100? 40?" He said, "Less than that."[9] Right after the second break Alex talks about the picture getting more clear as the truth about the wars come out. He talks about how the 25 Neocons who wrote PNAC were in high positions in the DOD and White House and Andreas von Bulow said "sure and part of them wrote the government program for Benjamin Netanyahu…"(Former Prime Minister of Israel). Alex goes on to ask who could have done this. Bulow said it was not the CIA and Alex jumps in saying so you're talking about black ops. Then Alex continues inferring, "We know only a MAJOR STATE could have carried this out?" Andreas says it must have been done from high up and it had to be done by a few people. Alex asks would you say 100–200, AVB says, "Less." Alex asks "50 people?" and AVB says "Less." I doubt that Alex could say it was the Zionists on the air, it would be career suicide. They were so close to saying it. A small group of Zionist Neocons (who were in the DOD and WHIG and wrote PNAC) with a state sponsor (Israel and the US) carried this out.

Journalists from the NY Times and CNN were purposely slipped information by Cheney's Chief of Staff, Lewis Libby.[10] Bush would say they would punish whoever was responsible, but later Libby named Both Bush and Cheney as the

---

8.   http://www.prisonplanet.tv/audio/200406vonbuelow.htm

9.   (To skip to this part, the marker on the QuickTime bar would be right in line with Andreas von Bulow's right ear)

10.   http://www.rys2sense.com/anti-neocons/viewtopic.php?t=550

people who authorized him to do it. Wow Bush has been caught lying again, what's new? Listen to what this lying hypocrite said. On September 30th 2003 after the kiss up press got done joking about Baseball, and asked Bush about the leaks, Bush said:

> *"And if there is a leak out of my administration, I want to know who it is. And if the person has violated the law, the person will be taken care of....I don't know of anybody in my administration who leaked classified information. If somebody did leak classified information, I'd like to know it, and we'll take the appropriate action."*
>
> *"I want to know the truth. If anybody has got any information inside our administration or outside our administration, it would be helpful if they came forward with the information so we can find out whether or not these allegations are true and get on about the business"*[11]

The nerve of Bush, of course he already knew who leaked the information because he was the one who authorized it! We now have Libby admitting that Bush and Cheney authorized him to leak the information.[12] This is yet another offense they could both be impeached for were we to have a functional republic. Libby was also a co-author of PNAC and worked with Paul Wolfowitz (captain Neocon now head of the WTO) under Cheney, in Bush the first's presidency. Interesting isn't it?

A ton of people simply can not accept anything that puts the blame on a religious minority because they have been conditioned and socialized into thinking that that is a form of hate or discrimination. We have Robertson and Falwell forking over Billions of tax free dollars to Israel. Forget about religion as a belief system for a minute and look at it as if it was a business. Ethnic and religious strife are nice buttons to push for a war. And if anyone opposes you then play the race card or the religion card on them, and accuse *them* of being the racist or the bigots. Zionists get to play the race card and the religion card to stifle any discussion about their illegal brutal military occupation of Palestine. If you were to say "write a paper about it," the MSM would be comparing you to David Duke by the next morning.[13]

Do not let them spin it. There is no way to justify bulldozing down homes to set up one's own racially segregated homes for JEWS ONLY. The Zionists are the racists and the real terrorists. Hamas can't hold a candle, to the fascist state of

---

11.   http://www.whitehouse.gov/news/releases/2003/09/20030930–9.html

12.   http://www.rys2sense.com/anti-neocons/viewtopic.php?p=8606#8606

13.   http://www.counterpunch.org/walt05052006.html

Israel, when it comes to crime and terrorism. But let there be no mistake about it, engaging in terrorism to fight terrorism is still terrorism. When these religious idiots go running with a bomb strapped to themselves and blow themselves up, often just killing innocent Jewish children, they are doing absolute evil, and they are not helping Palestine or any chance at peace one bit. (Warring statistics show that religiosity has been linked to religious terrorism.)

So Israel has been caught spying on the US **again**. What is new other than the fact that a foreign government can get caught spying in the US in a time of war and the Media will not report it. Just imagine if it had been Korean spies instead of Jews, and how big this story would be. Also imagine that we were attacking Korea's enemies and were following a war plan written off of Korean policy papers and a disproportionate number of the authors were all Korean Americans who were still in government and had dual citizenship with North Korea. Ha ha not a chance but you see Israel can get away with it because Israel is a cash cow for the Military-Industrial-Complex.

Corporations have obviously profiteered from the wars; this has been made quite clear. But did they write, implement, and use deception, to start this war or was that the Zionists? Who got caught spying on the US Halliburton or Israel? Israel that is who. The profiteering is a by product of the war as in any war. They are all in bed together because of overlapping interests between the military related corporations and the Zionists.

However, just how the Hell do they get away with it? Well they are free from any and all criticism because they play the two cards which an over-socialized liberal can not see through. They play the race card and the religion card, a double whammy. If you say the J word it is over, even if Israel has an illegal military occupation and sets up racially segregated colonies into Palestine, kills kids, knocks down the homes of civilians and attacks them with a military, and runs a brutal police state which is causing a backlash of terrorism on Israeli people (racist or not that is not a reason to kill someone). The Zionists are the real racist, engaging in ethnic cleansing in the name of defense and calling **any** opposition terrorists. They are creating terrorism by engaging in it themselves. Video link[14] Israel can do ANYTHING and the press will not mention it. But then again just who owns our press and our banks?...

The first oil pipeline negotiations for the oil in Iraq were between DC and Tel Aviv Israel. Here is where they planned it ten days before the end of the war.

---

14.   http://www.youtube.com/watch?v=RoWoQ9pqNbo

"Plans to build a pipeline to siphon oil from newly conquered Iraq to Israel are being discussed between Washington, Tel Aviv and potential future government figures in Baghdad.

The plan envisages the reconstruction of an old pipeline, inactive since the end of the British mandate in Palestine in 1948, when the flow from Iraq's northern oilfields to Palestine was re-directed to Syria.

Now, its resurrection would transform economic power in the region, bringing revenue to the new US-dominated Iraq, cutting out Syria and solving Israel's energy crisis at a stroke"-.[15]

And here is where they planned setting up another oil pipeline to Israel, this one going to Haifa.

"The United States has asked Israel to check the possibility of pumping oil from Iraq to the oil refineries in Haifa."

"The new pipeline would take oil from the Kirkuk area, where some 40 percent of Iraqi oil is produced, and transport it via Mosul, and then across Jordan to Israel."[16]

They are drooling over themselves to pump oil from Mosul to Haifa[17] Golly gee, that is interesting, why is all the oil going to Israel? Oh, it gets worse. The US sends oil to Israel from Iraq then buys it from Israel.

"One of Israel's largest oil marketing firms has won a multi-million dollar tender to supply fuel to US troops in Iraq. According to a IsraelNationalNews.com report, the tender awarded to Sonol gasoline company, along with its foreign partner Morgantown International, is valued at $70–80 million. The company is expected to supply the US forces with 25 million litres of fuel each month. The tender was issued by the US-based KDR Company, a subsidiary of Halliburton, which has been entrusted with the majority of US military contracts in Iraq."[18]*-Aljazeera*

---

15.   http://www.guardian.co.uk/Iraq/Story/0,2763,940250,00.htm
      Ed Vuillamy in Washington
      Sunday April 20, 2003 The Observer
16.   http://www.haaretz.com/hasen/pages/
      ShArt.jhtml?itemNo=332835&sw–Haifa і Mosul
          U.S. checking possibility of pumping oil from northern Iraq to Haifa, via Jordan
          By Amiram Cohen, Haaretz (an Israeli Paper)
17.   http://www.atimes.com/atimes/Middle_East/ED04Ak01.html

Well Israel did have an oil problem.

According to the Energy Information Administration (EIA), a statistical agency of the US Department of Energy, Israel produces almost no oil and imports nearly all its oil needs (around 237,000 barrels a day in 2002). Traditionally, major oil import sources have included Egypt, the North Sea, West Africa and Mexico."

"Information provided by the EIA states that in April 2003, there was some discussion of "reopening" the old oil pipeline from Mosul in Northern Iraq to the Israeli port of Haifa on its northern Mediterranean coast."

"The line, which was built in the 1930s, carried 100,000 barrels a day at its peak, but has been closed since Israel's establishment in 1948."[19]

The Mosul-Haifa pipeline is just the beginning. The plan is to take oil from Kirkuk where 40% of Iraq's oil is and Hafar al Batin, Al Basrah (Basara) and on top of Mosul. It all ends up in Israel. It's a war for oil the left shouts. "No blood for oil" they say. Yeh, that's true, 'no blood for oil' going to Israel, while our own gas prices rise and our soldiers get maimed and killed.

Now for more on 911. Back in Feb 2001[20] the US and UK attacked Iraq with much public Backlash. Bush bombed Baghdad just two weeks after being sworn in to office. He tried to start PNAC's plan then but the public was not having it. They needed that New Pearl Harbor event that PNAC said would be necessary. They rigged it with the Mossad's help on 911. There is a ton of disinformation about 911 from the likes of David Icke and the like, who talk about everything from human morphing reptilian space aliens to the secretive occult driven illuminati. This nonsense is a classic poisoning of the well, and hardly requires the consideration to even argue against it, but I wrote a blog about all the silly disinformation at this footnote[21] should anyone think it is necessary. The blackest lies are half a truth.

---

18. http://english.aljazeera.net/NR/exeres/14002292–509C–4896–951D–DAE550DFB88F.htm

19. http://english.aljazeera.net/NR/exeres/14002292–509C–4896–951D–DAE550DFB88F.htm

20. http://archives.cnn.com/2001/US/02/22/us.iraq.strike.02/

21. http://www.rys2sense.com/anti-neocons/viewtopic.php?t=1326

The Israeli connections are not widely mentioned in any 911 videos alternative radio and of course not on TV. Zionism is THE most sacred subject in the US. One mention of it and you are automatically and Anti-Semite. Well it is time to grow some balls and start talking about the Elephant in the room. Neocons from Israel and America started these wars and carried out 911. You know why Zionists are hated? No, it is not just their "we are the chosen race of god" religion. That grandiose dogma is no more asinine than any other religion. They are hated by Palestinians because the Israeli Army kills their kids, destroys their property, and makes them live in a Hell hole. THAT is why they are hated. And part of why we are hated too.[22] If America could only pry these parasite leeches off our back we could return to a respectable Jefferson worthy free republic.

---

22. http://www.informationclearinghouse.info/article13140.htm Video from a Iraq War Veteran admitting US war crimes.

32

Get Syria-s

The Neo-con spin about Syria has not stopped. Anyone familiar with the Israel "Clean Break"[1] scenario knows the phrase, "*The road to Damascus runs through Baghdad*". Three things come to mind in the war propaganda against Syria.

1. Moving WMD (Weapons of Mass Destruction)

2. Assignation of Hariri

3. Aiding the insurgency

As soon as the WMD in Iraq were nowhere to be found the Neo-con parrots and talking heads on TV started to 'suggest', with no evidence, that the weapons must have been moved[2] across the border to Syria. Ha, that makes sense. Have a war and have WMD, but don't use them against your enemy. Instead, get killed but hide your weapons just to make the US look bad. What a farce! Never mind the near impossibility of moving weapons into a different country, (who I guess, they would have us believe would just hold them for safe keeping). They would be moved under the watchful eye of satellites and in the middle of a war that they were hopelessly losing, where the western half which borders Syria was lost first.

Still this busload of baseless propaganda worked. I have heard many times, when arguing with Bush supporters, that the missing WMD were sent to Syria. Why now, would a country at war get rid of their best weapons when they had everything to lose? The US never had evidence of Iraq's WMD.

---

1. http://www.israeleconomy.org/strat1.htm
2. http://www.worldnetdaily.com/news/article.asp?ARTICLE_ID=36463 just one example

They claimed that Iraq did not comply with the UN resolution 1441, saying that they had not gotten rid of their Weapons of Mass Destruction. It was a modern witch trial, where Iraq had to prove they didn't have something. *You cannot prove a negative.* So since they did not turn in the weapons that they did not have (because that would be impossible) they were charged with not complying. Iraq did not have any WMD since the 1990s, when inspectors got rid of the last ones which our own country sold to them during Iraq's war with Iran.

Yes, that is dummy Rummy who has connections[3] to Dow Chemical, a chemical company involved in making the gas we gave them.

Back when Rafik Hariri was killed, the Neocons tried to pin it on the Syrians. They had a theory about a bomb placed under the road in an underground tunnel. The problem being that no underground tunnel existed, and then Ahmed Tayseer Abu Adas, took the blame/credit for the act.

Now we have a new attempt reaching for a pretext for Syria. We have increased tension on the Syrian border[4]. We have Israel periodically firing mortar rounds into Syria from the other side (which goes totally unreported in the US media) and now it looks like a stage is being set. The US will get into a 'shoot out' with Syrians or at least claim to, on the border of Iraq and Syria. Then one and two claims will be revisited by the Neo-con media. I'm sure Fox News will be foaming at the mouth.

If you think they are not crazy enough or dumb enough, to do this, I would like to remind the reader, that these are the same people who delayed helping hurricane victims for 5 days and then had the gall to try and rationalize it.

This time I don't think the public will fall for it outside of the 30% or so of born-again types who could watch Bush eat a baby on TV and find a way to rationalize it. But I also don't think public support is going to matter to the Neocons who live in their own world. (Bizzaro World[5]) Maybe they will stage another beheading or another CONUS attack. They always have a way to use scare tactics to sway the public herd into obedience. Maybe a famous sniper will be discovered to be from Syria or we will just cross over the boarder and attack them until they strike back which is when it will be reported that they struck first.

---

3.   http://www.guardian.co.uk/Iraq/Story/0,2763,866942,00.html
4.   http://www.wsws.org/articles/2003/jun2003/syri-j28.shtml
5.   http://www.antiwar.com/justin/?articleid=626

It now appears as though a faction from the OSP was sent to Iraq to PLANT Weapons of Mass Destruction. Larisa Alexandrovna reported:

""Three U.S. intelligence sources and a source close to the United Nations Security Council say that the Pentagon civilian leadership under the guidance of Stephen Cambone, appointed to lead Defense Department intelligence in March 2003, dispatched a series of 'off book' missions out of the ultra-secretive Office of Special Plans (OSP). The team was tasked to secure the following in order of priority: fallen Navy pilot Scott Speicher, WMD, and Saddam Hussein."[6]

"'They come in the summer of 2003, bringing in Iraqis, interviewing them,' the UN source said. "Then they start talking about WMD and they say to [these Iraqi intelligence officers] that 'Our President is in trouble. He went to war saying there are WMD and there are no WMD. What can we do? Can you help us?'

"The source said intelligence officers understood quickly what they were being asked to do and that the assumption was they were being asked to provide WMD in order for coalition forces to find them. 'But the guys were thinking this is absurd because anything put down would not pass the smell test and could be shown to be not of Iraqi origin and not using Iraqi methodology,' the source added."[7]

I had always wondered why they did not just plant some weapons and then 'discover' them. The 'off the book missions' were set into place, yet fortunately for truth, they failed. Amazingly it did not even seem to matter to the war-hawks who unconditionally support war when it serves as feel good machoism and vicarious power for the scared and prejudice.

With the up coming war with Iran and Syria, we must keep this in mind. Will the Zionist OSP plant some evidence to serve as a pretext for invading Iran? It is not beyond them. They lied about the Niger forgeries[8] which link right back up to Libby and the rest of the OSP. And we all know these cabals have rigged false flag operations before and have cooked up bogus intelligence in the recent past to justify their crimes.

---

6.   http://rawstory.com/news/2005/
      Secretive_military_unit_sought_to_solve_0105.html second paragraph
7.   http://rawstory.com/news/2005/
      Secretive_military_unit_sought_to_solve_0105.html 22d paragraph
8.   http://www.rys2sense.com/anti-neocons/viewtopic.php?t=550

Get out there an expose this. Blog away because the MSM is not going to report it. We have to become the media because basically we don't have one.

The Israelis were shadowing the patsies in 911. They lived next door to some of them. Five Israelis were dancing in the street after 911, and were arrested but they were released even though 2 of them were thought to be Mossad agents by the FBI. They had thousands in cash, box cutters, and maps of NY in their van which worked for a moving company in New Jersey which closed shop after 9–11 and the owner fled to Israel.[9].

"The five men—Sivan and Paul Kurzberg, Oded Ellner, Omer Marmari and Yaron Shmuel—were arrested eight hours after the attacks by the Bergen County, N.J., police while driving in an Urban Moving Systems van. The police acted on an FBI alert after the men allegedly were seen acting strangely while watching the events from the roof of their warehouse and the roof of their van." [10]

Interestingly, MSNBC reported police finding an explosive device on 911. Rick Sanchez reported that the police he talked to believed that an explosive device may have been planted in the World Trade Center in a van.[11] This live story was buried in the news and forgotten.

I wonder if it was a white van like the ones the Israelis were caught driving around in (who worked for a fake moving company in NJ) who were dancing and taking pictures of the burning towers with smiles on their faces. It looks more and more like an inside job for PNAC and Greater Israel. Israel has already been caught spying on us and having a large role in lying to us, to drag us into a war with Iraq. If you think the Likud Zionists had nothing to do with 911 then think again. They have a laundry list of false flag operations.

---

9.   http://www.whatreallyhappened.com/fiveisraelis.html

10.   http://www.forward.com/issues/2002/02.03.15/news2.html

11.   http://prisonplanet.com/video/051205explosives.wmv

33

Do you smell what I smell 911 and Israel.

Larry Franklin just so happened to be in Italy with Michael Ledeen on the same dates[1] that *someone* invented this bogus Niger-uranium claim. The OSP simply made this scare tactic up. Do you understand the level of censorship we have when a foreign government can be caught spying on the US who is at war, and none of the press will even mention it? Do you understand the severity of this, and how in the dark we could be about other matters, if we only relied on the MSM? Try to imagine if it had been a Korean spy ring.

1. What nation has made more nuclear weapons illegally than anyone else? And which country has thwarted America's nuclear deterrents in the past with a spy ring? (Google Jonathon Pollard)

2. Who had a spy ring in the DOD which fed top secret information to AIPAC? (Google Larry Franklin)

3. Why did his boss Richard Perle even have a job when he had been caught spying on the US in the 1970s for the same nation?

4. Why when our nuclear deterrents have been thwarted again does the media focus on Joe Wilson and not even mention the known spy ring in the DOD involving all the same people?

5. What nation wanted a war with Iraq and planned to use the US, and wrote about it in PNAC as well as in policy papers?[2] (cough cough "Clean Break[3]")

---

1.   Dec 2001
2.   http://www.israeleconomy.org/strat1.htm
3.   http://www.itszone.co.uk/zone0/viewtopic.php?t=38168

6. What nation has a religious/ethnicity claim to its country which Libby, Wurmser, Perle, Feith, Ledeen, Frum, Kristal, and a disproportionate number of the OSP belong to?

7. What nation is now calling for the US to attack Iran and Syria?

8. Five men from where were arrested on 911 dancing and taking pictures of themselves with the smoking towers in the backdrop?

9. Those same five men worked for a fake moving company in New Jersey a state whose governor was having a homosexual affair on his wife with a man from what country, who was appointed to head homeland defense for that state?

10. What country has been caught in the past committing terrorists' attacks on Egypt and Palestine and trying to blame it on Arabs?

11. Bush has met with the leader of which country more times than with anyone else?

12. What country gets more US aid than anyone else in the world?
    Give me an I, give me an S give me an R give me an A give me and E give me an L, What does that spell? ISRAEL! Do not say it too loudly though! It may be considered anti-Semitic to tell the truth or mention the facts.

Libby has been indicted and has resigned, but this is not over, and he is not just a sacrificial lamb, (as many pessimist believe) He is the war party's first casualty. More are coming. And DO NOT see this as the Left fighting back, the Left is as Neocon as the Right. This is Americans fighting back. Fitzgerald has openly stated he is an independent and it shows. Short of a mysterious plane crash or a freak suicide, this case is the War Party's undoing.

34

The race to Iran is against the AIPAC trial.

To reiterate, Larry Franklin the spy for AIPAC in the DOD had his trial on Jan 3d (2006) and he got 12 years in jail, which means he had to have made a plea bargain, because you get 20–40 or death for spying. The OSP wants to go to war with Iran before April because the trials from Steven Rosen and Keith Weissman are in April. Congress is voting on a nuclear option which is scary. They want to nuke a non-nuclear country.

The CIA can not prove that Iran does not have nukes anymore because the teams in charge of that had their cover blown when Lewis Libby (Cheney's Chief of staff) told reporters Judith Miller and Robert Novak the name of a clandestine agent named Valerie Plame. She worked for a front company called Brewster Jennings & Associates and so did many other agents all of whom were in charge with tracking nuclear weapons proliferation in the ME and Africa. Well when she was revealed, so was BJA and thus all the agents had to pull out. *I would not doubt it if dozens of people died from that but it is not like that would ever be reported on the news.*

The reason Libby narked on Plame was because either she or her teams could have proved that Iraq was not trying to buy Uranium from Niger Africa back in 2002–3. (*it had nothing to do with Joe Wilson which should be evident by the mere fact that the media reported on it.*) Bush got that intel not from the CIA but from a yet to be named Zionist (*a Karl Rove adviser named Michael Ledeen in my opinion*) who, as evidence is leaning, fabricated it in Italy with two former agents. However separate from that there were these bastards who were spying from inside the Defense department to pass info to Israel's lobby group AIPAC. They were gathering information about Iran's nuclear capacity, which as it turns out, is harmless (according to the IAEA international atomic energy agencies and also shared intel from European governments). They knew that by undermining our ability to check they would have enough fog of war to make their claims for Iran.

The FBI caught Frankilin on tape giving documents to AIPAC officials, Weissman was an Iran specialist and Rosen who was their top money man. Well both of these guys are squealing. They are even suing AIPAC because AIPAC fired them to distance themselves from the spies and to protect Israel. Libby has resigned and his old boss Perle and his under secretary Feith have ALL resigned. So basically. Come April, the whole world could find out that Israel has been spying on the US and a cabal of Zionists invented the BS that led us to war with Iraq and are also pushing for Iran. (Since the time of this writing the April court dated has been moved by the judge to May. And it appears that this date too will be bumped again to a later date.) They even wrote what they would do in 97 in policy papers called PNAC

35

Dissolving apathy.

o o o o o o o o o o o o o o o o o o o o o o o o o o o o o o o o
"Knowing is not enough; we must apply. Willing is not enough; we must do."

—*Goethe*

There are two main reasons an individual does not act. The first is that they feel like it is futile. The person thinks that their time could be better spent on monetary goals. Speaking out alone can feel like trying to hold back the tides. And to whom do you speak? How can you be heard? An individual can feel powerless. Knowing about things does not change them, only action does. "In her dreams her head was filled with wisdom and she awoke with the stinging realization that [alone] she had no way to share it or use it, and she regretted being awake." We are allowing personal comfort via constant distraction to be a blindfold for civic duty and social responsibility.

The belief that nothing can be changed is a self-fulfilling prophecy. It is one thing to provide new information to someone who unknowingly does wrong, for then they can change. But what can you say to those who knowingly do wrong? Or worse, what do you say to people who just do not care about anything that does not directly, immediately, and concretely affect them AKA disrupt their process of chasing shiny things? What motive does someone have to change when they do not care about right and wrong, when they only care about their own comfort level?

The second reason for apathy is that often there are no solutions available to a person, who has no voice, so why should they bother? For example, you see a war, you know it is based on lies, you can tell everyone you know and it won't matter.

You cannot fight the mass media. The mob is too busy to think, so they just put trust in 'their' leaders. Those not in the mob, are a minority that can be skipped over. An individual cannot fix the mob when they cannot reach the mob. Control of mass media means total control. So now we have a point of attack. The MSM is the flagship of the immoral and ignorant

We do not really have thinkers; we have herds; we have parties; we have ego-tribalism. Merit and precedence do not matter so much as pleasing fantasies and rationalizations. Hatred and fear bond the in-groups. Those too stupid to understand truth prefer a comfortable lie. When people are taught to fear ideas outside the herd, they hate them. The reason for rationalization is the fear of being wrong and the psychological enjoyment from the unification that comes from having a common feared enemy, like *reason*. Idiots are trained to rationalize, not to reason. Reason is scary because it requires freethinking, i.e. anti-authoritarianism.

But, a mind conditioned to accept obedience as virtue, cannot break away from authoritarianism. Desire, religion, hope, fear and prejudice are what color truth instead of knowledge. There is a system of control that breeds the unthinking yes-men; it is called religion—-a faith based system of judgment based on ignorance, fear, guilt, superstition, and dogmatism. Belief is all that is needed to make things true, even when they contradict other accepted beliefs. Because contradiction does not bother a religious mind, they can just ignore it or invent magical explanations or ad-hoc hypothesis.

One cannot use reason to argue with someone who has accepted magic because reason is already dead, especially when concepts of morality have been emotionally inner-mixed with the fairy tales. Make-believe means just what it sounds like, it means you have to make yourself believe it, i.e. lie to yourself.

Once people believe in a perfect source of information they can justify anything by claiming that this source wanted them to do, whatever it is that they themselves actually decided to do. Any crimes can, and have been, justified by dogmatic religious belief, from genital mutilation, to feudalism, from destroying information to murdering, burning women, committing suicide, waging war, refusing medicine, upholding slavery, animal sacrifice, and even genocide. The litany goes on.

People do not act, because they are waiting for an authoritarian voice to tell them to do so. They don't believe in things not handed to them by authority, "the news," "the book," "the leader."…They believe in chaos without a strong authority because that is all that pins down their own behavior.

"A full belly can not believe that hunger exist"—*Bruce Lee*

Knowledge does not seem to be the problem. Yes, there are people who honestly do not know about injustice. However, a far greater number are perfectly aware of things that they disagree with, from sweatshops to cigarettes. People know it is wrong to sell poison or exploit labor, but they let it go on in plain view, nothing is so important as to warrant disrupting their private comfort level.

Then, there are those who do want to change and are willing to sacrifice comfort but they have no direction. They have no idea what kind of realistic steps they could take to make anything happen. They don't act because others are not acting. The others are not acting for the same reason. So basically there are tons of people willing to act but they are all waiting to do it in unison, so that it will not be a waste of time.

Before the net we had no way of reaching one another but now we can organize ourselves to step out of line in greater numbers than ever before. Go be a leader, we have PLENTY of followers, go be the spark that starts a fire. Do not fear failure, fear inaction. People regret more what they wish they did than what they wish they did not do. Let us be relentless. The main stream media and the main stream or organized religions are clearly controlled by the government. Do not let them dictate what information you get or what your faith supposedly says you should think, do, and spend your money.

The hell with numbers! The numbers are there, they just need to see someone out there DOING something. The flocks will rise once someone shows that there is nothing to be afraid of so stand and be heard. Over half of this country is anti-war and that number is growing as people like us; continue to wake people up. We don't have to convert anymore people. We already are the majority. What we need is to get the people already against the war to **act**. Don't just protest Bush. It won't be covered. He can easily be replaced by some Neo-con Democrat, and nothing will change.

Protest the media. Let us start with Fox News and CNN. If either of those has outlets in your area, go there with a huge sign that says 'LIARS' because that is exactly what they are. Get on the web; it is the one place they have not monopolized yet. Join sites like www.anti-neocons.com (that is my site,) and help grass roots media. The more people who quit watching the lie box and stop reading the NY Times, the less money they make. As they keep losing money and audience to bloggers, they will start telling the truth more. For deep down their master is profit, and if we make truth telling profitable then they will do the right thing for the wrong reason.

Turn off your TV; it does not report the news anyway. You can order the sticker that is featured on the cover of this book and send it to your representative in congress. (www.myspace.com/rys2sense) If I were independently wealthy, then this book would be free. We have got to speak out, start with people in your own family.

The greatest way to prevent apathy is to not be apathetic. When you act others will follow. As Mark Twain once said,

"In times of change, the Patriot is a scarce man; brave, hated and scorned. When his cause succeeds, however, the timid join him, for then it costs nothing to be a Patriot."

We seem to be on phase three of what Mahatma Gandhi said,

"First they ignore you, then they laugh at you, then they fight you, then they win."

We are going to win. The Neo-cons are falling apart as I write. But if we are ever to prevent this kind of catastrophe from occurring again we have got to take back the media. The best way to do that is to support the creditable alternative media and more importantly to reject the establishment's media, **turn it off** and the green life blood called money, of their propaganda operation will halt and cause them to come crashing down.

The NWO cannot manipulate the public into its war games without the control of information. Now the internet has given a voice to a lot of kooks, and it seems to be mainly used for stealing music, shopping, and downloading porn. But, this foothold for freedom of speech has also allowed real patriots to expose the lies of the Neo-cons. Time has proven the predictive power of the bloggers and the deceptions of the MSM. People are turning to the web because they are sick of being lied to and the anti-neocon sites are tearing down the wizard's curtain.

There is no easy solution. But there are many things that would greatly reduce the power of these Neocons which can be done by ordinary citizens. First off, people can organize divestment campaigns with the churches or universities in their area. The divestment strategy is what helped to bring down the apartheid in South Africa. The Israel conflict in unquestionably one of the centers for milking money for the MIC. Some people said we went to war for corporate interest and some say it was a war for Israel and both arguments can be supported. Few have tied the two together to see how each feeds off of the other. THIS war party is so clearly made up of Zionists. But how many catch the overlapping interest of the corporations namely the largest one the MIC with the Zionists. These profiteers don't give a damn about Jews or anyone really, nor does the Lobby, they just care about money. However what safe guards them from criticism IS the religious angle. Corporations could not get away with it if they didn't have their all purpose shield of anti-Semitism around them and they would not have the hundreds of billions of dollars in extra backing from Christian religious factions. So it is multi-layered. It is not in America's or even the state of Israel's interests. It is in the interest of the Bankers and the corporate heads mainly from energy and defense industries who USE the Israeli conflict as their cash cow. They do the same thing with the Kashmir conflict only in that arms race between Pakistan and India they have predominately sided with the Muslims.

A divestment would take the money away from the companies who are involved in assisting the illegal Israeli occupation. This can be accomplished in a university by just a dozen hardworking activists. Many people are not even aware that there is an occupation; they believe the lie that Israel is merely defending itself from crazy suicide bombers yet they have no knowledge of Israel's crimes: massacres, the illegality, humiliation, brutality, and unapologetically racist occupation and settlements expansion. If companies like GE and Caterpillar have their investments pulled from them, they will listen, because where as ethics and morality fall on death corporate ears, money talks. A few Universities already have current divestment campaigns. UNC Chapel Hill, last year's NCAA champions, have a divestment campaign as do other prominent universities such as the University of California, Harvard-MIT, University of Illinois, University of Pennsylvania, Princeton University, Tufts University, Cornell University, University of Wisconsin and Bush's old school, where apparently he never learned how to use grammar, Yale University.

Religious organizations are another place to seek divestment. On February 6th 2006 The Church of England overwhelmingly voted to divest from Caterpillar for its involvement in home demolitions in Palestine.

"Campaigners today welcomed the Church of England's overwhelming vote in favour of divesting its 2.2 million shares from bulldozer manufacturer Caterpillar. The vote, supported by the Archbishop of Canterbury, Dr Rowan Williams, sends a clear message to Caterpillar that profiting from human rights violations is not compatible with socially responsible business practice.

The General Synod of the Church of England voted yesterday evening (6 February 2006) to disinvest from companies profiting from the illegal occupation, such as Caterpillar Inc, until they change their policies". The Church Commissioners now need to enforce the Synod's decision.

Caterpillar has been singled out by the United Nations for complicity in human rights abuses in the Occupied Palestinian Territories. Thousands of Palestinian homes and vast swathes of agricultural land have been destroyed by the Israeli military using armoured Caterpillar D9 bulldozers. "[1]

On election years you can try to vote for third parties especially on the local and state level. If you have a neocon as your representative then you have to work to get them out of there. These people are not going to change the only solution is to vote them out of office. Lastly if you got a good head on your shoulders run for your city council. Some races are won by only a thousand votes. Hardly anyone votes in these races and with some work you could win. We also have to support Anti-neocons like congressmen Ron Paul and R.M. Bowman who is running for congress in the 15 district of Florida this year. You have to speak out. If you believe that 911 was an inside job or that the government had foreknowledge then you need to say so. It has a snowballing effect. A lot of people share this position but they are afraid of being labeled as tinfoil hat wearers. As people stand up, more will follow. Like the JFK assassination the "conspiracy theorists" will become the majority. There is nothing wrong with believing in conspiracies when you have evidence. They have happened all through out history from the death of Julius Caesar to Jack Abarmoff, conspiracies happen in all nations all the time. To reject a theory simply because it involves a conspiracy is ludicrous. Even the official story about September 11th involves a conspiracy of 19 hijackers and a terrorists' network.

Get active, call in on radio shows and let them know your mind, the worst they can do is cut you off. Write something up for your local paper, the worse they can do is refuse to run it. Join the anti-war groups that are already out there like UFPAJ[2] or ANSWER[3]

There is a lot of disinformation floating around about 911. Stick to the facts. The scientific evidence shows that bombs were in the towers. The historical evidence of Neocons' PNAC and Israel's Clean Break Strategy together the current ongoing trials of Libby/Niger-gate/Plame and AIPAC/spy ring point give the motive for the attacks on Iraq which used 911 to ram through whatever legislation they wanted to get the wars they wanted. The wars are about control over economic resources and the fascists fantasies of Greater Israel. We know who deceived us into war, who was spying on us, who is calling for a war in Iran, who wrote this perpetual war agenda out over a decade ago, who enjoys a criticism free

1.   http://www.nosweat.org.uk/article.php?sid=1484
2.   United for Peace and Justice http://www.unitedforpeace.org/
3.   Act Now to Stop War and Racism http://www.internationalanswer.org/

media, and who has a cozy relationship with the MIC. All roads lead to Israel. And with that I believe you can conclude who was in on 911. The Anthrax letters made a telling projection when it said "Death to America Death to Israel" Because that is exactly who pulled off 911 and who is engaged in terrorism, torture, and preemptive warfare.

Write to your congressmen now http://www.house.gov/writerep/ Hand writing a letter is even better. An apathetic public begets an authoritarian government. If we do not get more active nothing is going to change. Next election vote against the incumbents regardless of their party unless you are one of the few who have an anti-war representative. The entire Republican Party aside from Ron Paul needs to go. R.M. Bowman of the 15th district of Florida is running, and I hope you will lend him your support. This is how a Democracy works. We have to support those who stand for liberty and toss out those who stand for profiteering, blind Zionism, and senseless war.

"War is over if you want it"-John Lennon

I leave you with a poem:

Plutocrats and Pawns ©

Poison my soul with the bravery of violence
Media control can kill truth with their silence
Mold our minds out of clay
Your bidding we will obey
The prestige we adore
Now give us now give us a war!

Fill me up, with lies I'm eager to identify
Ship me out, I am ready to kill or die
God's on our side so send us away
Kill for gold or oil it's the American way
Red skin or towel head
As long as they're all dead
It's a proud US tradition
To fill our greedy ambition
We'll pound'em to submission

With our bribed coalition
Now give us now give us our mission!

I won't believe the Bushit of the president
We must reform this money driven government
Destroy the two-party system, reclaim our land
No one will do it for you, you must make a stand.

Find a moral justification a reason for war
The public is hungry for the wargasm lore
An excuse to show our might, we will Shock and Awe
US's far right will subvert international law
Wave those flags high, like a mercenary whore
Concentrate the wealth while bleeding the poor
Now give us now give us some more!

I won't believe the Bushit of the president
We must reform this money driven government
Let's end the two-party system, reclaim our land
Will my fellow patriots lend me a hand?

Mr. TV said, we are fighting for liberation
Mr. Public said, amen, more ego-masturbation
Bang the drums, Bring On the occupation.
We're wrapped up in the movie, give us the glory
Uncritical of the hype, just feed us a story
Make lies fit our needs and the facts we'll ignore
Show images like a video game, edit the gore
Glory to our ego; kill the people 'Over There'
Just keep us afraid, we don't want to be aware
Now give us now give us a scare!

I won't believe the Bushit of the president
We must reform this money driven government

We should not support this two party sham.
But too many sheeple don't give a...

Mr. Bush said, they got weapons of mass destruction
And the OSP said, "Just follow our instruction!"
Eighteen thousand dead from gas, fire, and steel
Halliburton's sweat shops Must be worth the deal!
You got billion dollar unbidden contracts for rebuilding Iraq
Paid for with US taxes, corporate welfare is back.
Our domestic issues can wait, and the Bill of Rights can die
Killed by the Patriot Act, yet no one is asking why
Now feed us now feed us a lie.

I won't vote for Boy-George to be president
We must reform this money driven government
Destroy the two-party system, reclaim our land
No one will do it for you, you must make a stand

We got attacked on 911, but our foreign policy is not to blame
Abetting Israel's crimes against humanity is no need for shame
Make regressive taxes, and drive us into debt
Declare the war is over, and fly in on a fancy jet
Alienate our allies, with fourth Reich-wing legislation
Appoint your own committee for the 911 investigation
We got a War on education, and environmental disaster,
Plutocratic Tyranny has become our master

I won't assist the crimes of the president
We must reform this money driven government
The man can barely read who knows what he's thinking
There's lasting effects from 40 years of drinking

You said we were in danger, you said we must attack
I cannot subdue my anger; it will not bring my leg back
Spill our blood on the sand to bring profit for the Man
Now I can not stand, so your corporations could expand

Globalization all hail, you're a psychotic nut
I hope you land in jail, and take one in the…

But is this a Democracy or do we choose between the millionaires?
Just start a war; ignore the corporate scandals and mal-affairs.
Enron and WorldCom can get brushed under the rug
Just isolate Martha Stewart make **her** the big thug

You bomb civilian cities and that is morally OK
But gay-marriage should be outlawed? Is this the USSA?
You're a homophobic bigot, you claim Christianity
Your perversion of your religion is closer to insanity
God's on the money but this is not yet a theocracy
Money might be your god, but this is still a democracy

I won't promote the bigotry of the president
We must reform this money driven government
Complacent media is part of the scam.
But too many sheeple just don't give a…

It's the lesser of two evils, I too often hear
So choose your corporate puppet, it's election year
What do we get, when our government is up for rent?
We can't leave this fight to one outspoken guy from Flint
The party politicians and profiteers have no greater rejoice
Than to convince you with propaganda that they're your only choice
Now deny us, now deny us a voice

When the choices come down to only two, humanity or profit?
When neither shares your point of view, have the integrity to stop it
When both support a war that was backed by massive deception
Assuming that there is no foul play, and that we'll have a fair election

> If this is all that is left to choose from, then let it be said:
> I'm sorry America, but "Democracy is dead."

This was written on behalf of all the dead/wounded troops and their families, and all the Americans suffering under this money hungry inhumane president, his cabinet of liars, and the testosterone saturated chicken hawks playing cowboy, using nationalism as an extension of manhood. We do not have to be a culture ego-feeding itself with loosely rationalized violence. There is nothing glorious or noble about war. War is at best a necessary evil. Our nation is choking on Pentagon pork and a number of large corporate leeches sucking the blood of humanity and crapping out dollar bills. Authoritarian deception relies on Self deception. Wake up, stand up, and do not shut up.

Ryan 11–04–04

978-0-595-39384-8
0-595-39384-5

www.ingramcontent.com/pod-product-compliance
Lightning Source LLC
Chambersburg PA
CBHW020421290526
45785CB00002B/667